RETRO MANiA!

RETRO MANIA!

60 HIP HANDMADE CARDS, SCRAPBOOK PAGES, GIFTS & MORE!

by JUDI WATANABE,
ALISON EADS &
LAURIE DEWBERRY

NORTH LIGHT BOOKS

CINCINNATI, OHIO • WWW.ARTISTSNETWORK.COM

09 08 07 06 05   5 4 3 2 1

Distributed in Canada by Fraser Direct
100 Armstrong Avenue
Georgetown, ON, Canada L7G 5S4

Distributed in the U.K. and Europe by David & Charles
Brunel House, Newton Abbot, Devon, TQ12 4PU, England
Tel: (+44) 1626 323200, Fax: (+44) 1626 323319
E-mail: mail@davidandcharles.co.uk

Distributed in Australia by Capricorn Link
P.O. Box 704, Windsor, NSW 2756 Australia

Library of Congress Cataloging-in-Publication Data
Watanabe, Judi
    Retro Mania!: 60 hip handmade cards, scrapbook
pages, gifts and more! / Judi Watanabe, Alison Eads,
Laurie Dewberry.– 1st ed.
    p. cm.
    Includes index.
    ISBN 1-58180-746-5 (alk. paper)
    1. Greeting cards. 2. Paper work. I. Eads, Alison. II.
Dewberry, Laurie. III. Title.
    TT872.W37 2005
    745.594'1–dc22   2005010426

Editors: Christine Doyle, Tonia Davenport
Cover Designer: Karla Baker
Interior Designer: Terri Eubanks,
                   Leigh Ann Lentz
Production Coordinator: Robin Richie
Photographer: Greg Grosse
Photo Stylist: Nora Martini

METRIC CONVERSION CHART		
TO CONVERT	**TO**	**MULTIPLY BY**
Inches	Centimeters	2.54
Centimeters	Inches	0.4
Feet	Centimeters	30.5
Centimeters	Feet	0.03
Yards	Meters	0.9
Meters	Yards	1.1
Sq. Inches	Sq. Centimeters	6.45
Sq. Centimeters	Sq. Inches	0.16
Sq. Feet	Sq. Meters	0.09
Sq. Meters	Sq. Feet	10.8
Sq. Yards	Sq. Meters	0.8
Sq. Meters	Sq. Yards	1.2
Pounds	Kilograms	0.45
Kilograms	Pounds	2.2
Ounces	Grams	28.3
Grams	Ounces	0.035

MEET THE DESIGNERS

Judi Watanabe

Judi's love for card making started as soon as she was tall enough to reach the mail box. Learning to carve erasers led to her next passion—rubber stamping. Together with her husband, Rob, she grew JudiKins Rubber Stamps from a garage in 1989 to one of the most innovative craft product manufacturers in the industry today. Along with her corporate duties, Judi travels the world teaching and demonstrating rubber stamping techniques.

Alison Eads

As a self-proclaimed lover of "eye truffles" (like eye candy, only more so!), Alison has honed her style through years of interest in the creative and decorative arts. Alison is a designer and instructor for Scrapbook Central in West Chester, Ohio, and the author of *The Artful Card* (North Light Books).

Alison and her adorable husband, Charlie, call the Cincinnati area home. They have two practically perfect children and are busy living (mostly) happily ever after.

Laurie Dewberry

Laurie is a designer who, with her husband, Joel, has created a line of papers, templates and embellishments called The Paper Wardrobe (Plaid). She is an experienced party planner and the author of *Creative Wedding Showers* (North Light Books).

CONTENTS

10

SiGNED, SEALED, DELiVERED

MAKE SOMEONE HAPPY

28

44

BABY, iT'S COLD OUTSiDE

COME TOGETHER

56

74

MEMORIES ARE MADE OF THIS

LET'S GO RETRO!

Bright funky colors, bold designs, groovy lettering—what's not to love about retro? Everything old is new again—whether it's the hip sophistication of the 1940s, the lounge-chic feel of the 50s, or the free and loose styles of the 60s and 70s. And making cards, party favors and scrapbook pages with that retro appeal has never been easier.

Retro Mania! will show you how to create fabulous paper projects that evoke the looks of the past, while using all the fun papers, stamps and embellishments available in stamping and scrapbooking stores today. With step-by-step instructions, complete materials lists and lots of hints and tips along the way, you can make these same projects yourself or get inspired to create your own fun and funky designs.

Inside you'll find five swell sections to get your creative juices flowing. Signed, Sealed, Delivered showcases a few thank you's and lots of any occasion cards, like the Peace, Love and Flowers Card for your favorite hippie. In Make Someone Happy you'll find gifts for all your special someones including a gift can for a Groovy Gal and Hawaiian-inspired wine charms. Baby, It's Cold Outside is full of the holiday spirit, with cards perfect for the winter holidays of Christmas and Valentine's Day. The Come Together section will help you get the party rolling with invitations, decorations and favors for occasions like a Girly-Girl party or a Tragical Mystery Tour. Finally, in Memories are Made of This, you'll find scrapbook pages with a retro feel that celebrate school days, a 50s party, even your inner domestic diva.

So gather your paper crafting supplies, put on a pair of bell-bottoms to get in the mood, and go retro!

50s

60s

70s

thanks a

Lava!

9

SiGNED, SEALED, DELiVERED

Share the retro fun with the groovy gals and guys in your

life by creating these all-occasion cards. There's something

in this section for you, whether you're looking for a quick

card with a fabulous 50s look or a

special-occasion card for your favorite

flower child. And don't forget to say

thanks (or "Thanks-A-Lava") with a card.

Just seal with a kiss and send it on its way.

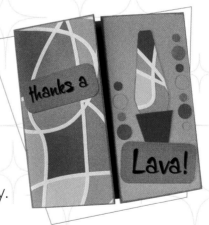

KISS ME KITTY CARD

Judi Watanabe

ALL I NEED

WHITE CARDSTOCK

KISS ME! STAMP
(JUDIKINS)

BLACK CAT STAMP
(JUDIKINS)

MOD CROWN STAMP
(JUDIKINS)

RETRO STARS STAMP
(JUDIKINS)

BOOMERANG PALETTE
STAMP (JUDIKINS)

POOL PALETTE STAMP
(JUDIKINS)

YELLOW-GREEN INK PAD

ORANGE INK PAD

LILAC INK PAD

BLACK PIGMENT INK
PAD

PINK INK PAD

BROWN INK PAD

Colorful and funky combinations of shapes and images are easy to achieve with a few rubber stamps and some ink pads. Pucker up!

1 Trim a piece of white cardstock to 5½" x 8½" (14cm x 22cm). Fold to make a 5½" x 4¼" (14cm x 11cm) card.

2 Stamp one boomerang in lilac vertically at the top of the card, and stamp one boomerang in yellow-green horizontally at the bottom left of the card. Both shapes should run slightly off the edges of the card.

3 Stamp the pool shape in orange at the bottom right of the card, overlapping the yellow-green shape. The pool shape should run off of the edge of the card.

4 Using black ink, stamp the kitty over the top of the orange pool shape, and stamp "Kiss Me!" slightly over the lilac boomerang shape. Give kitty a crown using the crown stamp and the pink ink pad.

5 Finally, randomly stamp three retro stars with brown ink.

GETTING CRAFTY

To make a crisp fold in a piece of paper, score it first with a stylus or a bone folder. Place your ruler on the paper and run the stylus or bone folder along the ruler. This compresses the paper fibers and makes it easier to fold.

Whether you take your martini shaken or stirred, you'll like making this swell card. There's just something fun about floating olives.

JAR OF OLIVES CARD

Judi Watanabe

ALL i NEED

BLACK GLOSSY CARDSTOCK

WHITE CARDSTOCK

SPOT DESIGNER'S BLOCK STAMP (JUDIKINS)

DOT STAMP

SMALL DOT STAMP

COCKTAIL BACKGROUND STAMP (JUDIKINS)

OLIVE GREEN INK PAD

YELLOW-GREEN INK PAD

RED INK PAD

CLEAR EMBOSSING INK PAD

CLEAR EMBOSSING POWDER

HEAT GUN

DOUBLE-SIDED TAPE

1 Trim a piece of black cardstock to 5½" x 8½" (14cm x 22cm). Fold to make a 5½" x 4¼" (14cm x 11cm) card. Trim a piece of white cardstock to 5½" x 2⅞" (14cm x 7cm).

2 Stamp the cocktail glasses image onto the left side of the black card, using clear embossing ink. Repeat the image, overlapping if necessary, to fill the length of the card. Don't worry about filling the portion on the right side—it will be covered up. Sprinkle clear embossing powder over the stamped images and tap off excess powder onto a piece of scrap paper. Funnel excess powder back into the jar. Heat the powder with a heat gun to melt it.

3 Stamp oval dots randomly over the white cardstock, using olive ink for the larger ovals and yellow-green ink for the smaller ovals. Create pimentos by using the red ink pad to stamp the larger dots over the olive green shapes and smaller dots over the yellow-green shapes.

4 Use double-sided tape to adhere the white cardstock to the right side of the stamped black card.

GETTING CRAFTY

Clear embossing ink and clear embossing powder are ideal for creating a subtle stamped image. It's particularly striking on black paper, but it looks great on paper of any color.

TALL & GROOVY CARD

Judi Watanabe

ALL i NEED

WHITE CARDSTOCK

TALL RETRO PALETTE
STAMP (JUDIKINS)

ATOMIC RETRO BOLLIO
STAMP (JUDIKINS)

YELLOW INK PAD

LIGHT GREEN INK PAD

BROWN INK PAD

Angular solid shapes in light colors form the background and set the mood for this retro card. Layer various light colors for an interesting effect. Funky-shaped teardrops, frames and ovals create patterns that can be used in a variety of groovy cards.

1 Trim a piece of white cardstock to 7½" x 8⅝" (19cm x 22cm) and fold to make a 3¾" x 8⅝" (10cm x 22cm) card. Stamp down the length of the card about 1" (3cm) from the right edge four times with the palette stamp. Alternate between yellow and light green inks, and vary the angle of the images slightly. (The images on either end should run off of the card.)

2 Using brown ink, stamp the bollio stamp down the center of the palette images, turning the stamp upside down when repeating the image.

Bold graphic shapes and a peek-a-boo layer of color give

this mod card a dramatic presence. You'll always have

a need for gender-neutral cards like this one,

so make a few while you're at it.

CUBiST iN COLOR CARD

Judi Watanabe

ALL i NEED

WHITE CARDSTOCK

GLOSSY BLACK
CARDSTOCK

CUBiST BLOCK STAMP
(JUDiKiNS)

ASSORTED CIRCLE AND
FLOWER STAMPS

BLACK PIGMENT INK
PAD

ASSORTED CHALK INK
PADS, SUCH AS LIME
GREEN, YELLOW, TEAL
AND CORAL

BLACK EMBOSSING
POWDER

CLEAR GLITTERY
EMBOSSING POWDER

HEAT GUN

DOUBLE-SIDED TAPE

1 Trim a piece of white cardstock to 7½" x 8⅝" (19cm x 22cm) and fold to make a 3¾" x 8⅝" (10cm x 22cm) card. Trim a piece of the black glossy cardstock to 3¾" x 1½" (10cm x 4cm). Stamp over the black piece with the block stamp and the black ink pad. You will need to stamp the image twice to fill the paper.

2 Sprinkle on the glittery embossing powder, tap off the excess and heat to melt with a heat gun. Adhere the embossed piece to the front of the card, centered horizontally, and 2¼" (6cm) from the top, using double-sided tape.

3 Randomly stamp a separate piece of white cardstock with the assorted circle and flower stamps and the colored chalk ink pads, overlapping some of the images. Let the ink dry.

4 Stamp over the colored images with the block stamp in black ink. Sprinkle on black embossing powder and heat to melt with the heat gun.

5 Trim the paper to the size of the embossed image and tape it to the front of the card, centering it on the black band.

ONE HiP CAT CARD

Alison Eads

ALL i NEED

SCRAPBOOK PAPERS:
  GROOVY RECTANGLES (SEI)
  PINK STARS (SEI)
PALE ORANGE CARDSTOCK
ORANGE VELLUM
KITTY RUBBER STAMP (HOT POTATOES)
ORANGE RHINESTONES, 5
ORANGE GLITTER
TANGERINE CHALK INK PAD
CHARCOAL CHALK INK PAD

SCISSORS
GLUE STICK
VELLUM TAPE
CRAFT GLUE
FONT: Doorkeeper

What's new pussycat? This mod kitty is purr-fectly groovy in her hip shades of pink and orange. A little sparkle from rhinestones adds just the right finishing touch.

1 Trim a piece of the pale orange cardstock to 5½" x 11" (14cm x 28cm) and fold to make a 5½" (14cm) square card. Trim a piece of rectangle paper to 5¼" (13cm) square and dip the edges into the tangerine ink pad. Using glue stick, adhere the paper to the front of the card.

2 Stamp kitty in charcoal ink onto the pink star paper. Dip the edges of the paper into the tangerine ink pad. Layer the stamped kitty onto the right side of the card, using glue stick.

3 Give her collar a bit of sparkle with some craft glue and orange glitter. Glue an orange rhinestone to the collar as well.

4 Print "You are the Hip-est of Cats" in the Doorkeeper font onto orange vellum. Trim the text to 3" x 1½" (8cm x 4cm) and, with vellum tape, layer it onto the bottom left of the card. Using craft glue, add an orange rhinestone to each corner of the vellum to finish.

MAKE iT RETRO

There are so many cool retro fonts out there, just begging to be used in your craft projects. Look for fonts at sites like www.fontdiner.com and www.1001fonts.com, or enter "retro fonts" into your favorite search engine.

Designing with geometric shapes in the
high-contrast combo of black and white came
into vogue in the middle of the 20th century.
The effect is just as stunning now as it was then.

GROOVY SQUARES CARD

Judi Watanabe

ALL i NEED

BLACK CARDSTOCK

WHITE CARDSTOCK

SQUARES EARTHQUAKE
STAMP (JUDIKINS)

BLACK INK PAD

BLACK EMBOSSING
POWDER

HEAT GUN

DOUBLE-SIDED TAPE

1 Trim a piece of black cardstock
to 8⅝" x 7½" (22cm x 19cm)
and fold to make a 3¾" x 8⅝"
(10cm x 22cm) card. Trim a
second piece of black cardstock
to 3¾" x 1¼" (10cm x 3cm).
Trim a piece of white cardstock
to 3¾" x 4¼" (10cm x 11cm).

2 Stamp the white cardstock and
the smaller piece of black
cardstock with the squares
stamp, using black ink.

3 Sprinkle on black embossing
powder and tap the excess
powder from each onto a piece
of scrap paper. Funnel
the excess powder back into
the jar. Heat the powder with
a heat gun to melt.

4 Tape the white cardstock to the
front of the card, placing it
about 1½" (4cm) from the top
of the card. Using more tape,
layer the small piece of black
cardstock onto the white
cardstock, 2½" (6cm) from the
top of the card.

GOTTA MATCH? CARD

Judi Watanabe

ALL I NEED

IVORY CARDSTOCK

BRONZE CARDSTOCK SCRAP

BEIGE CARDSTOCK SCRAP

Round Designer's Block circles stamp (JudiKins)

COPPER BRAD

BABY PINK CHALK INK PAD

BROWN CHALK INK PAD

MAGENTA CHALK INK PAD

STAPLER

BONE FOLDER

RULER

PENCIL

1/16" (2MM) HOLE PUNCH

1/2" (1CM) CIRCLE PUNCH

3/4" (2CM) CIRCLE PUNCH

Light a fire the next time you send a card with one made using this clever matchbook design.

The pages fit neatly inside, so that the cover can close just like a matchbook.

Making this card is even easier when you start with cardstock scrapbook papers, like these. (Rainbow Spiral from PSX and Little People from Colorbok)

1 Trim one piece of ivory cardstock to 2¾" x 9¼" (7cm x 23cm) and another piece to 2½" x 9½" (6cm x 24cm). On one side of the larger piece, randomly stamp with the circles stamp and the chalk ink pads. Make some of the circles go off of the edge of the cardstock, and overlap several of the circles.

2 Turn the stamped piece over and lay it horizontally. Use the pencil and ruler to make light marks along the top and bottom of the cardstock at these measurements from the left side: ¾", 1½", 5¼" and 5½" (2cm, 4cm, 13cm and 14cm). Use the bone folder and the ruler to score vertical lines at these marks, then fold the cardstock at the scored lines, making all folds go up from the stamped side.

3 Lay the smaller piece of ivory cardstock horizontally and again, using the ruler and a pencil, lightly make marks along the top and bottom of the cardstock at these measurements from the left side: 3½", 6¼" and 9¼" (9cm, 16cm and 23cm). Score vertically at all of these marks, and fold the cardstock accordion-style.

4 Lay the second piece so that the 3½" (9cm) segment is on your left, followed by two 3" (8cm) segments. Lay the stamped cardstock so that the two ¾" (2cm) segments are on your left. Center the smaller cardstock top to bottom on top of the front of the stamped cardstock and leave the left sides flush (the top cardstock will overhang the stamped cardstock on the right side). Staple the two pieces together at the center of the left edge.

5 Punch a ¾" (2cm) circle from the bronze cardstock scrap and a ½" (1cm) circle from the beige cardstock scrap. Using the ¹⁄₁₆" (2mm) hole punch, make a hole in the center of each circle. Punch a hole ⅞" (2cm) from the short side of the stamped cardstock, centered opposite the stapled end. Stack the circles and use the copper brad to attach them to the stamped side of the card.

6 Fold up the stamped cardstock to create a matchbook cover and fold the inner cardstock to fit inside of the cover. Insert the end of the cover under the folded flap to keep the booklet closed.

PEACE, LOVE & FLOWERS CARD

Alison Eads

ALL I NEED

SCRAPBOOK PAPERS:
FLOWERS ON WHITE (MARA-MI)
CHERRY BLOSSOM (MARA-MI)
RED FLORAL (MARA-MI)
BRUSH STROKES (WORDSWORTH)
PHOTO DAISIES (MASTERPIECE STUDIOS)
PAISLEY (ANNA GRIFFIN)
CORAL CARDSTOCK
INKJET TRANSPARENCY
WOODEN FLOWER
HOT PINK BUTTON
PINK AND ORANGE BRADS
PINK AND RED ACRYLIC PAINT
PAINTBRUSH
SCISSORS
ORANGE EMBROIDERY FLOSS
T-PIN OR NEEDLE TOOL
GLUE STICK
CRAFT GLUE
FONT: BERTHSIDE

The eye-popping colors and wild pattern mix on this card should appeal to any flower child, old or young. Although the patterns and mood of the papers are very different, they work together because they share the same vibrant colors. The message can be printed on a transparency (as shown) or directly on the paper.

1 Using the paintbrush, paint the wooden flower pink, let dry and then add a bit of red paint to the edges for an aged look. Set the flower aside to dry.

2 Trim a piece of coral cardstock to 10" x 7" (25cm x 18cm) and fold to make a 5" x 7" (13cm x 18cm) card. Cut scrapbook papers into strips of different widths and use glue stick to adhere them to the front of the card, in the following order (bottom to top): photo daisies, cherry blossom, brush strokes and flowers on white.

3 Print "Peace Love Flowers" on a transparency in a red-orange ink color. Trim to the width of the flowers on white strip and secure to the card with pink and orange brads. Use a T-pin or needle tool to create the holes first.

4 Cut out a flower shape, similar to the wooden flower, from the paisley paper. Cut a smaller flower from the red floral paper. Glue the small flower to the center of the large paisley flower and, using orange embroidery floss, sew the hot pink button in the center.

5 Glue the wooden flower to the left side of the card using craft glue. Layer the paper flowers on top of the wooden flower with craft glue to finish.

Keeping it simple is important when using a busy patterned image like this one. The texture of the embossing powder and the stark black and white palette combine to show off this design to high effect.

iN BLACK & WHiTE
CARD
Judi Watanabe

ALL i NEED

GLOSSY BLACK CARDSTOCK

WHITE CARDSTOCK

CUBIST BLOCK STAMP (JUDIKINS)

BLACK PIGMENT INK PAD

BLACK EMBOSSING POWDER

HEAT GUN

DOUBLE-SIDED TAPE

1 Trim a piece of glossy black cardstock to 5½" x 8½" (14cm x 22cm) and fold to make a 5½" x 4¼" (14cm x 11cm) card.

2 Using black ink, stamp the design on white cardstock. Sprinkle on black embossing powder and tap the excess onto scrap paper. Funnel the excess back into the jar. Heat the image with a heat gun to melt the powder.

3 Trim the image as close as possible to the outside border. Apply double-sided tape to the back of the white cardstock and adhere it to the front of the black glossy card. Place it so that the top and side borders around the block are the same.

METALLIC LAMPS
CARD
Judi Watanabe

ALL i NEED

WHITE CARDSTOCK

CLEAR ACETATE

SPOTS CUBE RUBBER
STAMP (JUDIKINS)

MOD LAMPS RUBBER
STAMP (JUDIKINS)

ASSORTED CHALK OR
PIGMENT INK PADS,
SUCH AS PERIWINKLE,
LIGHT BLUE, TEAL, LIME
GREEN AND MINT GREEN

BLACK PERMANENT INK
PAD

GOLD LEAFING PEN

TEAL AND SEA GREEN
METALLIC MARKERS

DOUBLE-SIDED TAPE

DIAMOND GLAZE
DIMENSIONAL ADHESIVE

Hanging accordion-folded paper lamps were a modern fixture in households of the 1960s. A new twist of metallic colors makes these retro-styled images fresh and interesting. Add a background of matching dots to make it extra groovy.

1 Trim a piece of white cardstock to 5½" x 11" (14cm x 28cm) and fold to make a 5½" (14cm) square card. Trim a second piece of white cardstock to a 4" (10cm) square. Use the spots stamp and the colored inks to randomly stamp dots over the entire surface of the 4" (10cm) square. Overlap many of the circles and run many circles off the edge. Keep one color for each size of the dots.

2 Layer the stamped piece onto the front of the folded card, centering it and adhering it with double-sided tape.

3 Trim a piece of the acetate to a 4" (10cm) square. Stamp the lamps image in black ink in the center of the acetate. After it has dried, turn the acetate over and use the leafing pen and metallic markers to fill in the lamps. Add gold dots to one of the lamps, and fill in around it with teal.

4 Apply a couple of dots of dimensional adhesive to the colored side of the acetate in the lamp areas and adhere to the stamped dots piece.

This cheerful card will chase away the blues for any down-and-out recipient. The supplies needed to send this sweet message are minimal so get going and make someone's day!

HAPPY CARD

Tonia Davenport

ALL i NEED

OLIVE CARDSTOCK

PINK CARDSTOCK

SCRAPBOOK PAPERS:
  Plot of Dots (SEI)
  Pretty Posies (SEI)

CARDSTOCK ALPHABET STICKERS (Aunt Gerti's Garden by SEI)

FLOWER STICKERS (Stickopotamus)

SCISSORS

PENCIL

WHITE COLORED PENCIL

FINE POINT BLACK MARKER

SABLE BROWN MARKER

GLUE STICK

1 Trim a piece of olive cardstock to 7" x 10" (18cm x 25cm) and fold to make a 7" x 5" (18cm x 13cm) card.

2 Trim a piece from the posies paper by starting at one straight edge and cutting a wavy line between a row of flowers, ending at the fifth flower. Cut around the fifth flower and continue diagonally up to the same edge of the paper that you started. Then from the spot where you first cut, measure up 3⅝" (9cm) and cut a horizontal line, perpendicular to the straight side. See photo as a reference.

3 Trim a 4" (10cm) square from the dots paper and cut a curve from one corner to the opposite diagonal corner. Glue the trimmed posies paper piece to the dots piece. Set the glued pieces on the top edge of the pink cardstock, and using a pencil, trace the hilly shape. Loosely cut out with scissors and glue all three pieces to the front of the card.

4 Using the fine point black pen, write the words, "don't Worry" on the pink cardstock. On a separate scrap of pink cardstock, write "be" and cut out the word in a tear drop shape. Color in the letters with the brown marker and then go over the letters with white pencil to soften.

5 Add letter stickers to spell "Happy" at the bottom of the card and glue the "be" shape over the *H*. Add a few flower stickers to the centers of some flowers. Cut two flowers from the posies scrapbook paper and glue to the top of the pink cardstock. See photo for placement.

ATOMIC FREEZE FRAME CARD

Judi Watanabe

ALL i NEED

WHITE CARDSTOCK

TURQUOISE CARDSTOCK

SELF-ADHESIVE CLEAR
LAMINATING SHEET

WINDOW PLASTIC

WHITE TASSEL

GREEN TASSEL

FUNKY FRAME STAMP

ASTRO ROCKET STAMP
(JUDIKINS)

FUNKY ATOM STAMP
(JUDIKINS)

BOLD SQUARES STAMP
(JUDIKINS)

ASTRO TWINKLE STAMP
(JUDIKINS)

RETRO STARS STAMP
(JUDIKINS)

SPOT DESIGNERS BLOCK FOR
DOTS (JUDIKINS)

BINK MARTIAN STAMP
(JUDIKINS)

RETRO ORNAMENTS STAMP
(JUDIKINS)

DOODLE STRINGS STAMP FOR
ROCKET LINES (JUDIKINS)

COLORED METAL FLAKES,
CLEAR GLITTERS, BEADS AND
CONFETTI

ASSORTED COLORED INK
PADS, SUCH AS LIME GREEN,
YELLOW-GREEN, LIGHT BLUE
AND LILAC

BLACK PIGMENT INK PAD

CHARCOAL GRAY INK PAD

SILVER GLITTER EMBOSSING
POWDER

SCISSORS

CRAFT KNIFE

CUTTING MAT

HEAT GUN

SMALL BRUSH

PENCIL

DOUBLE-SIDED TAPE

Based on "shaker" cards, this "freeze frame" card freezes the sparkle and glitz,

so you don't need to shake it up to see the sparkly bits.

1 Trim two pieces of the white cardstock to 5½" x 11" (14cm x 28cm) and fold each in half to make two 5½" (14cm) square cards. Trim another piece of white cardstock to a 2⅜" (6cm) square and a piece of turquoise cardstock to a 2⅝" (7cm) square.

2 Using the yellow-green, lilac and light blue ink pads, stamp one funky frame image of each color on the inside right side of one card. Placement can be random, but make sure the shapes overlap one another a bit. (See photo as a guide.) Working on a cutting mat, cut out the insides of the frames with a craft knife, being careful not to cut off the corners that protrude inside other frames.

3 Stack the stamped card on top of the other folded card and, with a pencil, lightly trace around the insides of the frames. Cut the traced shapes out with a craft knife, again, using the cutting mat.

4 From the laminating sheet, trim three 2" (5cm) squares, and from the window plastic, trim three 1¾" (4cm) squares. Peel the backing off of the laminating squares and sprinkle on colored metal flakes, glitters, beads and confetti, leaving a ¼" (6mm) border clear. Center one square of the window plastic over each embellished laminate square and press the two pieces together. Using the ¼" (6mm) adhesive portion that is still exposed, adhere the squares to the back of the stamped frames, trimming the plastic where images overlap, if necessary.

5 Apply double-sided tape to the back of the stamped card, running the tape around the plastic squares and around the perimeter of the card. Adhere the other trimmed card to the taped card, lining up the cut-out areas. Your card should now open up and have a windowed "page" inside.

6 On the last inside page of the card (the portion that shows behind the windows), stamp two rockets using the black pigment ink pad. When the ink is dry, use a brush and the light blue and yellow-green ink pads to color in the rocket shapes. Leave the window of the rockets without color. Stamp the elliptical row stamp (on the Retro Ornaments cube) in yellow-green, so that it runs off the bottom of the card, then stamp the martian head atop the row. Stamp one atomic image in charcoal gray ink beside one rocket.

7 Now open the card to the first two pages. Use the lilac, light blue, lime green and yellow-green inks to randomly stamp all three sizes of dot stamps, and use the charcoal gray ink to stamp the dots, stars and atoms. Be sure to have several images stamped off of the edge. Stamp one rocket in black ink on the left side, "traveling" toward the stamped frames. Stamp a curvy line with the Doodle String stamp in charcoal gray ink to trail from the back of the rocket.

8 In the center of the small white cardstock from step 1, stamp the squares stamp in yellow-green and let dry. Stamp the atomic stamp over the green squares. Sprinkle on glittery silver embossing powder and tap off the excess powder onto scrap paper. Funnel the excess powder back into the jar. Heat the powder with the heat gun to melt. Center the white cardstock square on the turquoise square (from step 1), using double-sided tape. Adhere the turquoise cardstock to the center front of the card using more tape. Finish the card by wrapping the white and green tassels around the spine of the back card and tie at the top.

Nothing says "retro" like a beaded curtain. This hint of a beaded curtain background with the bold block font creates a retro style that is fun and perfect for just about anyone.

THANK YOU! CARD
Judi Watanabe

ALL I NEED

BLACK CARDSTOCK

WHITE CARDSTOCK

RETRO THANK YOU STAMP (JUDIKINS)

BEAD CURTAIN BACKGROUND STAMP (JUDIKINS)

OLIVE INK PAD

LIGHT PURPLE INK PAD

LILAC INK PAD

BLACK INK PAD

CLEAR EMBOSSING INK PAD

CLEAR EMBOSSING POWDER

HEAT GUN

DOUBLE-SIDED TAPE

1 Trim the black cardstock to 5½" x 11" (14cm x 28cm) and fold to make a 5½" (14cm) square card. Stamp onto the left side of the card with the clear embossing ink and the beaded curtain stamp, and sprinkle on clear embossing powder. Tap off excess powder onto a piece of scrap paper. Funnel excess powder back into the jar. Heat the powder with a heat gun to melt the powder.

2 Trim a piece of white cardstock to 5½" x 4¼" (14cm x 11cm). Stamp the light purple ink pad directly onto the top center of the white cardstock, extending the pad over the edge of the card just a bit. (The white cardstock and the ink pad should both be vertical.) Stamp the lilac pad to the right of the light purple and the olive to the left. Stamp the lilac, horizontally at the bottom of the olive and light purple shapes. Stamp the olive pad, vertically, next to the lilac, extending down off the bottom edge of the card. Finally, fill in the remaining areas with olive on the left and light purple in the center. Use the photo as a guide if needed.

3 Over the entire surface of the white cardstock, stamp the beaded curtain with clear embossing ink. Sprinkle on clear embossing powder. Tap off excess powder onto a piece of scrap paper. Funnel excess powder back into the jar. Heat the powder with a heat gun to melt the powder. Stamp "Thank You!" in black ink at the top half of the card. Tape the stamped piece to the right side of the folded card to finish.

THANKS-A-LAVA
CARD
Alison Eads

ALL i NEED

PATTERNED SCRAPBOOK PAPER (KI MEMORIES)
WATERMELON CARDSTOCK
RED CARDSTOCK
ORANGE CARDSTOCK
WATERMELON CHALK INK PAD
SCISSORS
1/4" (6MM) CIRCLE PUNCH
1/2" (1CM) CIRCLE PUNCH
GLUE STICK
PATTERN ON PAGE 90
FONT: CHARADE

There's just something about lava lamps that brings a smile to your face. How about a bubbly card in hot shades for a friend who has made you smile?

1 Trim a piece of watermelon cardstock to 6" x 12" (15cm x 30cm). Create a gatefold card by folding in the card at 3½" (9cm) on either end of the cardstock. Trim a piece of both the orange cardstock and patterned paper to 5⅞" x 2⅞" (15cm x 7cm). Dip the edges of both pieces into the watermelon chalk ink pad. Using glue stick, adhere the orange piece to the front right flap and the patterned paper to the front left flap.

2 Cut out a lamp base from the red cardstock and a lamp from the scrapbook paper, using the pattern. Dip the edges of the lamp into the watermelon ink pad. Glue the pieces of the lamp to the center of the orange cardstock.

3 From a scrap of patterned paper, punch several circles of color, using the two circle punches. Alternating ¼" (6mm) circles and ½" (1cm) circles, glue the "bubbles" in two rows up either side of the lamp. You may wish to dip the orange-colored circles into the ink pad first, to provide more contrast against the orange cardstock.

4 Print "thanks a" and "Lava!" onto watermelon cardstock, in the Charade font. Trim the pieces to fit the card, and round the corners using scissors or a corner rounder punch. Adhere the "thanks a" piece to the left flap at an angle, and the "Lava!" piece to the right flap at the opposite angle.

MAKE SOMEONE HAPPY

Receiving a gift always makes someone happy, but receiving a

gift in a cool retro theme is simply tops. In this section, you'll find

gifts for any occasion. Celebrate birthdays with the Groovy Gal

Card and Gift Can, wedding showers with the Grandma's

Recipes Envelope Book, or a

housewarming with the Taste of the

Tropics Glass Charms. Don't miss

your chance to make someone happy

with a fun and funky retro gift.

Recipes

Main Course

Desserts

SUGAR HONEY CAKE
1 cup Brown sugar
2 cups White sugar
stir 4 tablespoons honey
together! ½ cup milk
enjoy! 1 tsp baking powder

Dreamy frosted
fruit
3 oz heavy whip

GROOVY GAL
CARD
Laurie Dewberry

ALL i NEED

SCRAPBOOK CARDSTOCK PAPERS:
  Groovy Diamonds (SEI)
  Groovy Mini Dots (SEI)
  Pink Slippers solid pink (SEI)
  Groovy Grass green stripes (SEI)
WHITE CARDSTOCK

DIMENSIONAL ADHESIVE DOTS
GLUE STICK
FONT: Sparkly

Say "happy birthday" in style with this groovy card and gift can (next page). Giving a card a retro feel can be as easy as using funky shapes and fonts!

1 Print the words "Happy" and "Birthday" on the green striped cardstock. Cut words in retro-shaped rectangles (about 2¾" x 1¼" [7cm x 3cm]). See pattern on page 90.

2 Adhere the trimmed text to white cardstock, using glue stick, and trim to leave ⅛" (3mm) on all sides.

3 Fold a 7½" x 5" (19cm x 13cm) piece of the pink cardstock in half, then cut the card into a retro-shaped rectangle, wider at the top and narrowing to the bottom (or use the pattern on page 90).

4 Trim a row of about four diamonds from the diamonds paper, and trim the sides to match the bottom of the card. Adhere to the bottom of the card with glue stick.

5 Cut a strip of dots from the dots cardstock, and trim it to go at the top of the diamonds. Adhere the strip with glue stick.

6 Mount the word rectangles on the card with dimensional adhesive dots.

As a gift to go with the card on the opposite page, this groovy can is filled with bath items and other goodies. A magnet for the fridge will keep the recipient happy all year round.

GROOVY GAL
GIFT CAN
Laurie Dewberry

ALL i NEED

HALF-GALLON PAINT CAN

SCRAPBOOK CARDSTOCK PAPERS:

   POGO STICKS STRIPES (SEI), 2

   GROOVY GRASS GREEN STRIPES (SEI)

   TAN-A-RAMA SOLID TAN (SEI)

WHITE CARDSTOCK

STICKER PAPER

CLEAR GLASS MARBLE WITH FLAT BACK

ROUND MAGNET

CLEAR-DRYING SUPER GLUE

SPRAY ADHESIVE

GLUE STICK

FONT: SPARKLY

1 Cut the two sheets of the multi-colored striped paper to the height of the can. Spray the two pieces with spray adhesive and wrap them around the can, smoothing out any bubbles.

2 Print "Groovy Gal" onto the sticker paper, using the Sparkly font and trim to 3½" x 2" (9cm x 5cm). Peel off the backing and mount to the tan cardstock. Trim the tan paper down into a retro rectangle shape (or use the pattern on page 90.)

3 Adhere the trimmed label to the can, using spray adhesive or glue stick, and add a retro-shaped rectangle, cut from the green striped cardstock, using glue stick.

4 Print "Smile" on a piece of white cardstock and cut to fit the glass marble shape. Here, I jazzed my text up with a funky white and pink flower on a grass green background.

5 Adhere the marble over the word with super glue. Add a round magnet to the back with the same glue.

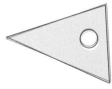

GETTING CRAFTY
Using the sticker paper, add matching labels to homemade bath salts or other items that will go into the gift can.

STARLET'S BATH SALTS
GIFT BOX
Alison Eads

ALL I NEED

PAPIER MÂCHÉ ROUND BOX,
4 1/2" X 2 1/2" (11CM X
6CM)

SCRAPBOOK PAPERS

  PINK FLORAL (RAINBOW
  WORLD/MASTERPIECE
  STUDIO)

  PINK WATERCOLOR
  (AUTUMN LEAVES)

  PINK STRIPE (SUSAN
  BRANCH-COLORBOK)

WHITE CARDSTOCK

PINK SILK ROSEBUD

PINK SATIN CORD

ROSE-COLORED WIRED
RIBBON, 1 1/2" (4CM)
WIDE

SCISSORS

1/8" (3MM) HOLE PUNCH

5" (13CM) CIRCLE TEMPLATE
OR COMPASS

PENCIL

GLUE STICK

CRAFT GLUE

FONTS:

  A&S BLACK SWAN

  NEW YORKER

This gift box was inspired by advertisements in the 1940s for luxurious beauty products used by Hollywood starlets. Using the same product as a favorite star was a way to claim a little of that glamour for oneself. Fill the gift box with bath salts, shimmery powder or other small, glamourous gifts.

1 Trim one piece of the pink floral paper into two 2½" (6cm) wide strips. Apply glue stick to the back of one piece and adhere it around the perimeter of the box. Trim the second piece to fit the gap left by the first and adhere with glue stick. Trace the box onto the floral paper, and cut out the circle, slightly smaller than where you traced. Glue this circle to the bottom of the box with glue stick.

2 Using either a circle template or a compass, draw a 5" (13cm) circle onto the pink watercolor paper and cut it out with scissors. Cover the top of the lid with glue stick and center the circle on the lid. Use scissors to snip little flaps into the paper that overhangs the lid, making the cuts about ½" (1cm) apart (it will look like fringe). Glue the flaps down to the side of the lid with glue stick.

3 Cut two ⅝" (2cm) strips from the striped paper. Glue one strip around the perimeter of the lid, covering the snipped flap pieces. Trim the second piece to fill the gap left by the first and adhere with glue stick.

4 Tie a big foofy bow around the box using the rose-colored wired ribbon.

5 For the gift tag, trim a piece of white cardstock to 4¾" x 3¼" (12cm x 8cm), and fold it in half to make a tag. Trim a piece of the pink striped paper to 2⅜" x 3¼" (6cm x 8cm) and use glue stick to adhere to the front of the tag.

6 On a piece of the pink watercolor paper, print a "product" name and description. Trim the piece to make a 2" x 2½" (5cm x 6cm) oval label, apply glue stick to the back and center it to the front of the tag. Use craft glue to add the silk rose to the corner of the tag.

7 Punch a hole in the top left of the tag, using the ⅛" (3mm) hole punch, and tie the tag onto the bow with pink satin cord.

This card was inspired by old motel signs, particularly those glitzy numbers in Las Vegas. The sparkle, flamboyance and magnitude of those signs is a fitting tribute for the birthday of someone pretty special.

A FABULOUS BiRTHDAY CARD

Alison Eads

ALL i NEED

SCRAPBOOK PAPERS:
  BeBopNBeads (SEI)
  BLUE BANGLES (KI MEMORIES)
OLIVE CARDSTOCK
RED CARDSTOCK
PALE BLUE CARDSTOCK
YELLOW-GREEN CARDSTOCK
CIRCLE TEMPLATE

SCISSORS
1/4" (6MM) CIRCLE PUNCH
GLUE STICK
CRAFT GLUE
FONTS:
  A&S Bone Casual
  A&S Black Swan

1 Fold a piece of 7" x 10" (18cm x 25cm) olive cardstock in half to make a 5" x 7" (13cm x 18cm) card. Trim a piece of the beads paper to 6¾" x 4¾" (17cm x 12cm) and, using glue stick, center it on the front of the card.

2 Cut a 1½" x 4½" (4cm x 11cm) rectangle from the olive cardstock, and cut the center out of it to form a *U* shape. Adhere to the front of the card, left of center.

3 Print "Fabulous Birthday you deserve it!" onto pale blue cardstock. (See photo for approximate point size differences.) Print all text in black.

4 Trim the text into the shape of a diamond. Round the two side corners with scissors. Glue the diamond to the card, using glue stick. Center it side to side and just a bit higher than center top to bottom.

5 Punch circles from the yellow-green cardstock with the ¼" (6mm) circle punch. You'll need about 45 or so. Using dots of craft glue, glue the circles around the perimeter of the diamond.

6 Leaving ample space between each letter, print "have a" onto the blue bangles paper.

7 Using a circle template, trace a circle around each letter, varying the placement of the letters inside the circles. Cut out the circles and glue onto the top portion of the card.

8 Cut an eight-pointed star shape from the red cardstock and adhere to the top left of the olive rectangle shape. Trim points that go over the fold to be flush with the card.

PRECiOUS PiNWHEELS

Judi Watanabe

ALL i NEED

DECORATIVE PAPERS
SUCH AS RAINBOW
SPIRAL (PSX), SOLID
SEVENTIES
(MASTERPIECE),
STRIPES
(PROVOCRAFT) OR
PAPER YOU'VE
STAMPED

SMALL DIE-CUT
FLOWER OR OTHER
EMBELLISHMENTS

RULER

PENCIL

CRAFT KNIFE

CUTTING MAT

1/8" (3MM) HOLE
PUNCH

1/8" (3MM)
EYELETS

EYELET SETTER

HAMMER

THUMB TACKS

1/4" (6MM)
WOODEN DOWEL

CRAFT GLUE

Pinwheels blowing in
the breeze are always
a simple way to make
someone smile, and
with fresh flashes of
retro colors and
patterns, these are
especially appealing.

1 Cut a piece of scrapbook paper to a 7" (18cm) square. (Increase or decrease the size of the square for larger or smaller pinwheels.) Using the ruler and a pencil, draw two diagonal lines from corner to corner.

2 From the center of the square, where the lines cross, make a mark with the pencil at ½" (1cm) on each of the four lines. With the paper on a cutting mat, cut along each of the lines, using the ruler and a craft knife, from the ½" (1cm) pencil mark to each of the corners.

3 Punch a hole at the center mark of the the paper with the ⅛" (3mm) hole punch. Also punch a hole to the right of each line in the corners, about ⅛" (3mm) from the corner point and centered between the cut edge and the outside edge.

4 Roll each punched tip to the center and insert an eyelet from the back of the paper (at the center hole) to the front and through all four of the punched tips. Set the eyelet from the front, using an eyelet setter and a hammer (see page 89 for instructions).

5 Secure the pinwheel to the dowel by pressing the thumb tack through the eyelet hole and into the wood.

6 Cover up the tack by gluing a flower cut from a coordinating piece of paper (or other embellishment) onto it with craft glue.

Next time you give someone a housewarming gift, make it a warm Hawaiian welcome with this card and the tropical glass charms on the next page. Tropical motifs came into vogue in 1959 when the Hawaiian Islands became the 50th state in the Union.

iSLAND iDOL
CARD
Judi Watanabe

ALL i NEED

WHITE CARDSTOCK

SCRAP PAPER

HAWAIIAN PRINT
STAMP (JUDIKINS)

TIKI IDOL STAMPS
(JUDIKINS)

COCONUT PALM TREE
STAMP (JUDIKINS)

KHAKI INK PAD

BROWN INK PAD

SCISSORS

DOUBLE-SIDED TAPE

1 Trim a piece of white cardstock to 5½" x 11" (14cm x 28cm) and fold to make a 5½" (14cm) square card. Trim a second piece of white cardstock to 5½" x 3¼" (14cm x 8cm). On the front of the folded card, stamp the Hawaiian print stamp in brown ink. Stamp along the folded edge and the opposite edge.

2 In the center of the smaller piece of white cardstock, stamp a row of the four Tiki idol images, using brown ink. To create a mask to protect the images, stamp them again, in the same order and the same spacing, on a piece of scrap paper. Cut out the images with scissors, leaving the idols connected at the top, to make things easier.

3 Set the mask over the previously stamped Tiki idols on the white cardstock. Ink up the palm tree stamp with khaki ink and stamp repeatedly over the white cardstock to fill in all of the white space. Hold the mask with one hand as you stamp.

4 Remove and discard the mask. Using double-sided tape, adhere the idol and palm trees piece to the center of the card. The fold should be at the top of the card.

TASTE OF THE TROPICS GLASS CHARMS

Judi Watanabe

ALL i NEED

TRANSPARENT SHRINK PLASTIC

SAND CARDSTOCK

LARGE PALM TREE STAMP (JUDIKINS)

PALM FROND STAMP (JUDIKINS)

BISMARK PALM STAMP (JUDIKINS)

BANANA TREE STAMP (JUDIKINS)

UKULELE STAMP (JUDIKINS)

PRESSED FERN STAMP (JUDIKINS)

HAWAIIAN PRINT STAMP (JUDIKINS)

ASSORTED SILVER, GOLD AND COLORED GLASS BEADS

HOOP EARRINGS, GOLD OR SILVER, 3 PAIRS

JUMP RINGS, 6

GREEN INK PAD

BROWN INK PAD

SAND INK PAD

BLACK INK PAD

COLORED PENCILS

1/8" (3MM) HOLE PUNCH

SCISSORS

PENCIL

RULER

CRAFT KNIFE

CUTTING MAT

BAKING PARCHMENT

COOKIE SHEET

Along with the Island Idol Card on the previous page, these glass charms make a festive gift for housewarmings, birthdays and or any occasion that could use a little taste of the tropics.

1 Stamp the images onto a sheet of transparent shrink plastic, using green, brown and black inks. For the trees, ink the foliage portions with green ink and trunks with brown ink, then stamp the images. Set the sheet aside to dry.

2 Cut the images out with scissors and color in the images with colored pencils. Using the ⅛" (3mm) hole punch, punch a hole at the top of each trimmed image, about ¼" (6mm) from the edge.

3 Set the images on a piece of baking parchment on a cookie sheet, and bake in a 300°F (150°C) oven for a few minutes until the pieces flatten. Remove from the oven and press flat while they are still warm with the flat side of a large wood-mounted stamp or similar object.

4 Attach a jump ring to each image. To assemble each wire charm, open up an earring, thread on one metallic bead, a glass bead, another metallic bead, the jump ring on the shrink plastic image, a metallic bead, glass bead and final metallic bead. Repeat for the remaining five hoops and charms, matching bead color to each individual charm as desired.

5 Set the hoops aside and begin creating the gift card. Trim a piece of sand cardstock to 5½" x 8½" (14cm x 22cm) and fold to make a 5½" x 4¼" (14cm x 11cm) card.

6 Stamp on the front of the card with sand ink and the Hawaiian print stamp. You will need to stamp three horizontal bands to fill the card. It's fine to have the images overlap slightly, and they should all go off the edges of the card.

7 Open the card up and turn it face down. On the back of the stamped side, use a ruler and pencil to mark three ¼" (6mm) squares ¼" (6mm) from the top of the card, in a horizontal row. Then make a second row of three squares, 2¾" (7cm) from the top (see template on page 91). Set the card on a cutting mat, and use the craft knife to cut three sides from each marked square. (Leave the side toward the fold line uncut.)

8 Turn the card back over so that the stamped side is up. Bend each of the squares toward the fold, and punch a hole in the center of each one with the ⅛" (3mm) hole punch. Attach one hoop to each little flap to finish.

MAKE iT RETRO

Looking for some retro inspiration? Old magazines are a terrific source for getting the look and feel of a bygone era. The photography and advertisements are sure to get your creative juices flowing. Stop at your used bookstore to see if there's a stack of magazines tucked away in a corner somewhere. Or check out your local antique mall—there's usually at least one vendor who has a collection of magazines full of hidden treasures.

JET SETTER JOURNALS

Judi Watanabe

ALL i NEED

COMPOSITION BOOK

PALM TREES PAPER (CREATIVE IMAGINATIONS), 2 PIECES

COORDINATING SOLID COLOR CARDSTOCK

METAL LABEL HOLDER

DECORATIVE BRADS

RULER

PENCIL

SCISSORS

BRUSH FOR GLUING

BONE FOLDER

BRAYER

AWL

CRAFT GLUE THINNED SLIGHTLY WITH WATER

MASKING TAPE

A mechanism for keeping track of addresses and dates that doesn't require batteries? You can't get more retro than that! Change a boring composition book or calendar into retro-styled creations by covering them with your favorite mod papers.

1 Measure the front cover of the composition book, *not* including the black spine portion. Cut a piece of scrapbook paper ½" (1cm) wider and 1½" (4cm) longer than the cover. Place a strip of masking tape over the black spine. Spread a thin layer of glue over the front of the cover with the gluing brush.

2 Carefully lay your trimmed piece of paper onto the cover, centering it top to bottom, and butting it up against the taped spine. Smooth out the paper with your hand, then use a brayer to thoroughly remove any bubbles.

3 Open up the cover so that the glued paper is face down. Use scissors to snip two cuts at each rounded corner of the overhanging paper. Make the cuts approximately where the curve starts and stops. Using a gluing brush, apply glue to all the overhanging paper and fold it over onto the inside of the cover. Burnish the edges and rounded corner with a bone folder. Repeat steps 1–3 for the back cover.

4 On the front of the journal, position the metal label holder where you would like it, and mark where the holes are on the cover with a pencil. Slide the cutting mat under the front cover and make holes at the marks, using an awl. Attach the label holder to the cover with the decorative brads, inserting the brads through the holes created.

5 Trim two pieces of solid cardstock to fit the inside of the front and back covers. The paper should butt up to the inner pages but be about ⅛" (3mm) smaller than the cover on the outside edges.

6 Spread glue over the trimmed cardstock and adhere one piece to the inside of each cover. Add a printed label to the holder on the front to finish.

POCKET JOURNAL

ADDRESS BOOK

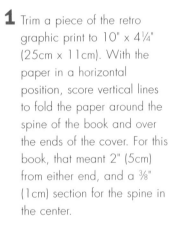

1 Trim a piece of the retro figures paper slightly larger than the entire cover of the journal (in this case 6½" x 4¾" [17cm x 12cm]). Use the gluing brush to apply glue to the entire outside of the cover. Smooth the trimmed paper over the cover, working out any bubbles with your fingers.

2 Open up the cover flat on a cutting mat and trim the excess paper carefully along all four sides of the cover, using a craft knife.

3 Trim a piece of the metallic paper 2" x 4½" (5cm x 11cm). Use an awl to poke three holes along one long edge of the metallic paper for the brads. Insert the flanges of a star into each hole and spread the flanges to secure.

4 Apply adhesive to the back of the paper and adhere it around the spine of the journal, centering it front to back.

1 Trim a piece of the retro graphic print to 10" x 4¼" (25cm x 11cm). With the paper in a horizontal position, score vertical lines to fold the paper around the spine of the book and over the ends of the cover. For this book, that meant 2" (5cm) from either end, and a ⅜" (1cm) section for the spine in the center.

2 Using craft glue, glue the black ribbon along one of the short sides of the paper, centering it over the paper.

3 With the paper folded in the shape of the book, slide the book cover into the flaps of the folded piece. Tie the ribbon ends into a bow to secure the cover.

GRANDMA'S RECIPES ENVELOPE BOOK

Judi Watanabe

ALL i NEED

#6 3/4 ENVELOPES, 6	FINE-POINT BROWN MARKER
3" X 5" (8CM X 13CM) INDEX CARDS	PENCIL
WHITE CARDSTOCK	BONE FOLDER
ASSORTED RETRO STAMPS, SUCH AS	RULER
RETRO STARS (JUDIKINS)	1/8" (3MM) HOLE PUNCH
BOOMERANG PALETTE (JUDIKINS)	1/8" (3MM) EYELETS, 2
RETRO TRIANGLE PALETTE (JUDIKINS)	EYELET SETTING TOOL
TALL RETRO PALETTE (JUDIKINS)	PROTECTIVE SURFACE
SKYLARK CUBE RETRO SHAPES (JUDIKINS)	HAMMER
RETRO CLIP ART FIGURES	SCISSORS
CHALK INK PADS IN ASSORTED COLORS, SUCH AS MAGENTA, TANGERINE, BROWN AND OLIVE	DECORATIVE TWINE, 10" (25CM)
	GLUE STICK

With recipes for everything from household cleaning solutions to Grandma's famous pickles, recipe cards have been shared and copied for years. This envelope portfolio provides a snappy new way to share and store your favorites from yesterday. Bon appétit!

1 Trim a piece of white cardstock to 6¾" x 10¼" (17cm x 26cm). Decorate one side of the cardstock using the chalk inks and assorted stamps. Stamp small retro shapes in two separate colors on a scrap of cardstock and cut out the shapes with scissors. Set these shapes aside.

2 Turn the stamped side of the cardstock face down. With the piece in front of you horizontally, make marks lightly with a pencil on the top and bottom edge of the cardstock, starting from the left side, at the following measurements: 1⅞", 3¾", 4⅛", 8" and 8⅜" (5cm, 10cm, 11cm, 20cm and 21cm).

3 Use the bone folder and a ruler to score vertical lines at each of the connecting marks. Fold and crease the cardstock at each of the scored lines, making all of the folds in the same direction, to create a portfolio.

4 The end that has a 1⅞" (5cm) segment will be the top of the portfolio and has an extra flap folded toward the inside for added stability. With this flap folded in, punch a hole with the ⅛" (3mm) hole punch through both layers, about ½" (1cm) from the folded edge and centered side to side.

5 Punch another hole in the other end of the cardstock about 1" (3cm) in from the edge and off center (either direction). Punch holes in the two cut-out shapes from step 1. Using the eyelet setting tool, hammer and protective surface, attach these shapes to the stamped side of the portfolio with eyelets.

6 Tie the decorative twine around the shape on the bottom flap and trim to hide the short end. The length can now be used to wrap around the top shape to close the portfolio. Set the portfolio aside.

7 For the inside of the portfolio, first create an accordion with the envelopes by adhering the back of one envelope to the inside of the flap of a second envelope, using glue stick. Continue stacking the six envelopes. Adhere the front of the flap of the top envelope to the inside center panel of the portfolio. The envelopes will be folded in alternate directions to fit inside the portfolio.

8 Use assorted stamps, ink pads and 50s hostess clip art figures to decorate the envelopes, including the back of the bottom envelope. Use a fine-point brown pen to write "Recipes" on the front cover, next to the closures. Write "Appetizers," "Beverages," "Main Course" or other categories you choose on the fronts of the envelopes.

9 Decorate the index cards with the same stamps and inks, keeping the imagery around the outside of the cards and insert a couple into each envelope to serve as recipe cards.

ALL iN THE FAMiLY
JOURNAL
Laurie Dewberry

ALL i NEED

Debossed Daisies Cardstock (SEI)

Double-Sided Scrapbook Cardstock:

- Antique Stripe (SEI)
- Robin Egg (SEI)
- Dainty Dots (SEI)
- Oven Mitts (SEI)
- Debossed Dots (SEI)
- Table Ticking (SEI)

White Cardstock

Mat Board

Brown Ribbon, Granny's Kitchen Notions Pack (SEI)

Labels and Tabs, Granny's Kitchen (SEI)

Craft Knife

Cutting Mat

Brayer

Bone Folder

1/8" (3mm) Die Hole Punch

Hammer

Spray Adhesive

Glue Stick

Each year at Christmas time our family exchanges stories we remember about one another. I created this journal to give to each family member so they will have a place to put all of those cherished memories.

1 Cut pieces of the following size from the mat board using the craft knife and a cutting mat: 9" x 9" (23cm x 23cm), a 10⅛" x 9" (26cm x 23cm) and 1" x 9" (3cm x 23cm) piece.

2 Cut two pieces of the daisies paper to 11⅛" x 10" (28cm x 25cm). Spray one side of the larger piece of mat board with spray adhesive and adhere it to the center of one of the pieces of paper. Turn the board over and press the paper down well with a brayer. Spray the 9" (23cm) square piece of board with adhesive and adhere it to one end of the other piece of paper, so that there is a 1" (3cm) border on three sides, and a 2⅛" (5cm) border on the fourth side. Spray the last strip of board and adhere it next to the square piece, with ⅛" (3mm) of space between the two board pieces. Turn over and brayer down well.

3 Using scissors or a craft knife, cut off the corners of the paper of both mounted pieces at a 45° angle, leaving about 1⁄16" (2mm) of space between the corner of the board and the cut edge of the paper. Apply glue stick to the overhanging paper on all sides and wrap around and secure to the backs of the boards. Use a bone folder to burnish the paper to the edges of the board.

4 Use the bone folder to burnish an indent on the front of the piece that has two sections of board, to make it easier to fold up. You may need to push the two pieces together to be able to work the bone folder into the groove without tearing the paper.

5 Affix a 10" x 8⅞" (25cm x 22.5cm) piece of the striped paper to the inside of each cover with spray adhesive. Bend the front cover piece at the groove to loosen up the paper at the fold before the glue dries completely.

6 Using the hammer and punch, make holes 1¼" (3cm) from the top and bottom and ½" (1cm) in from the sides of both covers.

7 Choose coordinating papers of your choice for the divider pages of the book and trim to 8⅞" x 9½" (22.5cm x 24cm). Select divider tabs and mount onto each of these pages.

8 Cut pieces of white cardstock to 8⅞" x 9" (22.5cm x 23cm) to serve as the journal pages. Use one cover as a guide to mark where you will punch holes.

9 Use the hole punch and hammer (or a hand-held punch) to punch holes through the journal pages and divider pages to match the covers.

10 Thread the ribbon though each of the holes in the back cover, then through all the inside pages and out through the holes in the front cover. Tie a bow to keep the pages in place.

11 Select a label from the coordinating tags and labels and adhere to the front lower right corner with glue stick.

MAKE iT RETRO

Black-and-white photos give your projects a retro feel no matter when they were taken. And taking black-and-white photos has never been easier. If you have a digital camera, your photos can be printed in black-and-white or even in sepia by a film processing lab or on your own computer printer.

For those without the hi-tech gadgetry, black-and-white film is available for your regular camera, and it's processed just like color film, so there's no extra time or charge involved. You can even get one-time-use cameras with black-and-white film! Now that's cool.

BABY, IT'S COLD OUTSIDE

The cold, gray winter months are the perfect time to
pull out your crafting supplies and retro papers to create
chic and stylish holiday cards. In this
section you'll find quick rubber-stamp
Christmas cards you can make for
everyone on your card list and pretty
Valentine's Day cards perfect for that
special sweetie in your life.

SNOW PARTY CRACKERS

Alison Eads

ALL i NEED

4 1/2" (11CM) CARDBOARD TUBES (SUCH AS TOILET PAPER OR TRIMMED-DOWN PAPER TOWEL)

IVORY GIFT TISSUE

SCRAPBOOK PAPERS:
  BROWN STRIPES (MUSTARD MOON)
  BLUE HARLEQUIN (CREATIVE IMAGINATIONS)

RED CARDSTOCK

SHEER IVORY RIBBON

LIGHT BLUE RICKRACK

RED GROSGRAIN RIBBON

RETRO SNOWMAN MAGNETS

SCISSORS

SCALLOPED-EDGE SCISSORS

GLUE STICK

TRANSPARENT TAPE

A 40s-fresh color scheme of pale blue, cranberry, chocolate and ivory will liven up any holiday celebration. Invite friends over for sledding and serve hot chocolate and cookies. When it's time for guests to depart, send them home with a holiday cracker filled with goodies.

1 Make snowman images to allow one image per cracker, or purchase snowman magnets like used here. Trim the images with scissors, if needed, and set aside.

2 Fill empty cardboard rolls with candy, treats or small gifts.

3 Trim gift tissue to approximately 8" x 12½" (20cm x 32cm). Stack three layers of tissue together and center a filled tube at one end of the stack (there should be just over 4" [10cm] of tissue on either end of the tube). Roll the tube up in the three layers of tissue and secure with a piece of transparent tape.

4 Using scissors, fringe the ends of the tissue by cutting parallel strips about ½" (1cm) wide. Tie the tissue at the ends of the tube with sheer ivory ribbon, tying in a knot to secure. Then tie rickrack over the ivory ribbon. Repeat steps 3 and 4 for the remainder of the tubes, tying some of the tubes with red grosgrain ribbon.

5 Now you are ready to layer the red cardstock and two scrapbook papers over the tubes. Trim some of the striped paper and some of the red cardstock to 4½" x 8" (11cm x 20cm) and wrap the tubes with one or the other, securing the ends of the papers with glue stick. Next layer varying widths of 8" (20cm) long blue harlequin paper over the first layer on the tubes, again securing with glue stick.

6 Trim an assortment of 8" (20cm) long striped paper, red cardstock and blue harlequin papers to a smaller width, trimming some of the 8" (20cm) sides with the scalloped-edge scissors. Layer these pieces over the first two layers and secure with glue stick.

7 Apply glue to the backs of the magnets or trimmed images and center one on each of the tubes to finish.

MAKE iT RETRO

You'll find retro images are everywhere once you're on the lookout

for them. They're on stationery and note cards, even home decor items.

For retro images you can use in your artwork, look online for

copyright-free pieces. You'll find loads of web sites for retro clip art—

just type in "clip art + retro" in any search engine, or check out sites

like www.havanastreet.com and www.retroart.com.

And many stamp manufacturers are creating cool retro designs that

you can use as well, so be sure to check out your local stamp store.

COOL YULE CARD
Judi Watanabe

ALL I NEED

WHITE CARDSTOCK

BOOMERANG PALETTE STAMP
(JUDIKINS)

RETRO TRIANGLE PALETTE STAMP
(JUDIKINS)

THIN LINES CUBE STAMP FOR STARS
(JUDIKINS)

COOL YULE STAMP (JUDIKINS)

YELLOW-GREEN INK PAD

LIGHT PURPLE INK PAD

TEAL INK PAD

BLACK INK PAD

CLEAR EMBOSSING POWDER

HEAT GUN

SCISSORS

Geometric shapes and
asterisk-type stars give this
holiday card its retro style.
Play with the inks you
choose, overlapping them
to create different shades
that enhance the mood.

1 Trim a piece of white cardstock to 5½" x 8½" (14cm x 22cm) and fold in half to make a 5½" x 4¼" (14cm x 11cm) card. Stamp the boomerang stamp in teal at the bottom left of the card. Stamp the triangle palette in the right center in light purple and stamp it again at the top left in yellow-green. Let dry.

2 Stamp "Have a Cool Yule!" in black ink at the bottom right of the card. Sprinkle on clear embossing powder, tap off excess onto scrap paper and funnel it back into the jar. Melt the powder with a heat gun.

3 Using black ink, stamp one retro star to the left and slightly above the embossed phrase and stamp a second star at the top right of the card to finish.

Surprise everyone with a bright and colorful Christmas greeting with a twist.

Changing the color scheme from the traditional makes this retro-style card fresh and hip.

XMAS GREETINGS CARD

Judi Watanabe

ALL I NEED

WHITE CARDSTOCK

TALL RETRO PALETTE STAMP (JUDIKINS)

POOL PALETTE STAMP (JUDIKINS)

FIFTIES VEGETATION CUBE STAMP (JUDIKINS)

RETRO STARS STAMPS, THREE IMAGES (JUDIKINS)

TIFFANY CAPS ALPHABET STAMPS (JUDIKINS)

YELLOW INK PAD

ORANGE INK PAD

PINK INK PAD

BROWN INK PAD

1 Trim a piece of white cardstock to 5½" x 8½" (14cm x 22cm) and fold to make a 5½" x 4¼" (14cm x 11cm) card. Using pink and orange inks and the vegetation, stamp a row of building images across the bottom of the card, alternating colors. The angle and spacing of the images should be somewhat random. The images should run off each side of the card.

2 Stamp the pool image in pink on the right side above the building row. Stamp the tall retro image horizontally in yellow, centering it side to side and between the top of the card and the building row.

3 Using brown ink and the alphabet stamps, stamp the word "Greetings" in the center of the yellow image. Stamp the retro stars in brown ink randomly over the card, using a total of five stars.

ALUMINUM TREE CARD

Alison Eads

ALL I NEED

SILVER CARDSTOCK, SCREEN-TEXTURED

AQUA PEARL CARDSTOCK

TURQUOISE METALLIC, HEAVY-TEXTURED CARDSTOCK

SILVER PIPE CLEANERS

GLASS BEADS, AQUA AND GREEN TONES

SCISSORS

CRAFT GLUE

GLUE STICK

FONT: Fontdinerdotcom

Remember aluminum trees? This cool card pays homage to that unforgettable holiday icon of the 1960s. (They always looked a little Charlie Brown-ish to me.) The metallic silvers and blues are all in keeping with the "modern" look.

1 On a piece of aqua pearl cardstock, print "Have a Cool Christmas!" in the Fontdinerdotcom font. Trim the piece so that the text is at the bottom and the finished size is 3½" x 5" (9cm x 13cm). Round the corners of the piece, using scissors or a corner rounder punch.

2 Using glue stick, adhere the text piece to the textured turquoise cardstock. Trim, leaving ³⁄₁₆" (5mm) of the turquoise cardstock on all sides (finished size will be 3⅞" x 5⅜" [10cm x 14cm]). Trim the silver cardstock to 6" x 8½" (15cm x 22cm) and fold to make a 6" x 4¼" (15cm x 11cm) card. Adhere the layered pieces to the front of the silver card, using craft glue.

3 To make the tree, cut silver pipe cleaners into graduated lengths. Twist the middle of each row of branches around a piece that will serve as the trunk. The trunk here is 4" (10cm) long, and the horizontal branch rows are 3", 2½", 2¼", 1¾" and 1" (8cm, 6cm, 5.5cm, 4cm and 3cm).

4 Place a dab of craft glue onto the ends of the branches and slide on the beads. Glue the tree to the front of the card, centered above the text, using craft glue.

This cute little kitty just says "I'm adorable."

Because this kitty is a rubber stamp, you can

change the ink colors and use it again for spooky

Halloween cards. Now, that's the cat's meow.

VALENTINE KITTY
CARD
Judi Watanabe

ALL i NEED

RED CARDSTOCK

WHITE CARDSTOCK

Fab Heart stamp (JudiKins)

Black Cat stamp (JudiKins)

Swirly Happy Valentine's Day stamp (JudiKins)

MAGENTA INK PAD

PEACH INK PAD

BLACK INK PAD

DOUBLE-SIDED TAPE

1 Trim a piece of red cardstock to 8½" x 7½" (22cm x 19cm) and fold to make a 8½" x 3¾" (22cm x 10cm) card. Trim a piece of white cardstock to 3¼" x 6" (8cm x 15cm).

2 Using magenta ink, stamp the heart once at the top left of the white cardstock. Stamp the heart again in peach ink at the center right of the cardstock, just overlapping the point of the magenta heart.

3 Stamp "Happy Valentine's Day" in the center of the white cardstock, using black ink. Stamp the kitty at the bottom center of the white cardstock, in black ink.

4 Apply double-sided tape to the back of the white cardstock and adhere to the front of the red card, centering it side to side and place it ½" (1cm) from the top of the card.

GETTING CRAFTY

Cleaning your stamps the right way helps to keep them in good shape. Use a stamp cleaning product that you can get at any craft or stamping store and just follow the directions. When you're using the same stamp in multiple colors, like for this card, clean the stamp if you're going from a dark color to a light. It's not usually necessary if you go from light to dark.

A CLASSIC COUPLE
VALENTINE
Alison Eads

ALL I NEED

SCRAPBOOK PAPERS:
  PINK HARLEQUIN (PSX)
  GREEN SWIRLS (CAROLEE'S CREATIONS)

PINK CARDSTOCK

1960S ROMEO AND JULIET VALENTINE

TINY GOLD FRAME

GOLD HEART BUTTON

SHEER GREEN RIBBON

APPLE GREEN CHALK INK PAD

PINK GLITTER

SCISSORS

RULER

PENCIL

CRAFT GLUE

GLUE STICK

FONT: DOORKEEPER

What could be more classically romantic than Romeo and Juliet? This mod pair comes from a vintage Valentine, but you can get your own retro imagery from clip art sites (see Make It Retro on page 47) or from stacks of retro greeting cards at your local thrift store or antique mall.

1 Fold a piece of 8" x 9¼" (20cm x 23cm) pink cardstock in half to make a 4" x 9¼" (10cm x 23cm) card. At the bottom of the front of the card, layer a strip of the green swirl paper that is the width of the card and about 1½" (4cm) high, using glue stick.

2 Trim two pieces of the pink harlequin paper to the width of the card. One piece should be 8½" (22cm) long and the other 2" (5cm). Using scissors, cut a loose scallop design along one edge of each of the pieces. Edge each scallop with craft glue and pink glitter (see photo as a guide). Adhere the larger piece to the front of the card, using glue stick. Glue the smaller piece at the top, leaving the scallop portion glue-free so that you can insert the Valentine underneath it.

3 Trim a piece of the green swirls paper to 3¾" x 4" (9.5cm x 10cm). Setting the paper at a slight angle, layer it onto the front of the card, with the top under the pink scallop, using glue stick. Trim any excess paper that extends over the sides of the card.

4 Place the vintage Valentine on the front of the card at an angle. The top left corner can be under the top pink scallop. Using a ruler and pencil, lightly mark lines at the edges of the card and trim the excess. Dip the edges of the trimmed Valentine into the apple green ink pad then, using glue stick, layer it over the top of the green swirls paper.

5 Print "we're a classic couple" on pink cardstock and trim it to the size of the tiny gold frame. Adhere the text to the front of the card, using glue stick, then glue the frame onto the text with craft glue.

6 Tie a bow with the sheer green ribbon. Using craft glue, glue the bow and the heart button to the front of the card, below the frame.

MAKE iT RETRO

What was the style in the 60s? Just about everything, according to Joy Shih in her book *Funky Fabrics of the Sixties*. Pastels were left over from the 50s and were turning to more earthy colors at the beginning of the 60s. By mid-decade, floral and paisley designs were all the rage, in bright neon and psychedelic colors. By the end of the 60s, hot shades of yellow and orange had taken over and carried through into the 70s.

SCHOOL SWEET-HEART VALENTINE

Alison Eads

ALL I NEED

SCRAPBOOK PAPERS:

WRITING PAPER (KAREN FOSTER DESIGN)

BLACK AND WHITE CHECK (FRANCES MEYER)

RED CARDSTOCK

1940S VALENTINE, COLOR COPY (TIMBUCKTOO PRODUCTIONS)

HEART-SHAPED BUTTONS

BLACK EMBROIDERY THREAD AND NEEDLE

SCISSORS

GLUE STICK

CRAFT GLUE

Remember making Valentines in grade school? The lined paper we used to practice our writing brings back the fun as a background for a sweet vintage Valentine.

1 Trim a piece of red cardstock to 6" x 12" (15cm x 30cm) and fold to make a 6" (15cm) square card. Trim a piece of the writing paper to a 5¾" (14.5cm) square.

2 Using glue stick, adhere the writing paper to the center of the red cardstock. Trim a piece of the checks paper to a 3¾" (10cm) square and center it over the writing paper using glue stick.

3 Trim the image from the Valentine using scissors, and adhere it with glue stick to the center of the checks paper.

4 Using a needle threaded with black embroidery thread, pull the needle from the back of each button, to the front, and back down through the other hole to the back. Tie off the thread in a knot at the back and trim the thread close to the knot. Using craft glue, adhere the three heart buttons, evenly spaced at the bottom of the card.

Here's a Valentine with a twist. Instead of the usual card format, this love note is wrapped around an empty ribbon spool. Secured with a red ribbon, it's a Valentine your honey is sure to remember.

SCHOOL SPOOL
VALENTINE
Alison Eads

ALL i NEED

EMPTY RIBBON SPOOL

SCRAPBOOK PAPERS:

WRITING PAPER (KAREN FOSTER DESIGN)

BLACK AND WHITE CHECK (FRANCES MEYER)

RED PAISLEY PAPER (PRINTWORKS)

RED FLOWERS (KAREN FOSTER DESIGN)

1940S VALENTINE, COLOR COPY, REDUCED (TIMBUCKTOO PRODUCTIONS)

HEART-SHAPED BUTTON, YELLOW BUTTON AND BLACK BUTTON

BLACK EMBROIDERY THREAD AND NEEDLE

RED SATIN RIBBON, 1/2" (1CM) WIDE

BLACK BRAD

SMALL ALPHABET STAMPS

BLACK INK PAD

CREAM ACRYLIC PAINT

PAINTBRUSH

PENCIL

SCISSORS

GLUE STICK

CRAFT GLUE

1 Using cream acrylic paint and the paintbrush, paint the inside of the empty ribbon spool. Set aside to dry.

2 Trace the spool onto the writing paper, using a pencil, then cut out the circle with scissors. Glue the circle to the top of the spool, using glue stick. Repeat for the bottom of the spool, using the red flowers paper.

3 Using scissors, cut out the Valentine. Glue it to a 2" (5cm) square of the checks paper. Then glue the layered square onto the writing paper on the spool with glue stick.

4 Thread the needle with black embroidery thread, then thread it through the holes in a button and tie off in the back. Repeat for each button. Attach the buttons to the bottom left corner of the layered Valentine square with craft glue.

5 Cut a ½" x 9½" (1cm x 24cm) strip of paisley paper and, using glue stick, glue it around the inside of the spool, leaving ½" (1cm) or so at the end loose.

6 Cut a ½" x 12" (1cm x 30cm) strip of the writing paper and stamp a message onto it, using the small alphabet stamps and black ink. Glue one end to the back of the free end of the paisley paper on the spool.

7 Trim another piece of the paisley paper to ½" x 1½" (1cm x 4cm) and fold in half. Glue this piece to the free end of the stamped paper, using glue stick. Cut a length of the red satin ribbon to about 26" (66cm). Fold the ribbon in half, and attach the center of the ribbon to the paisley tab using the black brad. Roll the message up around the spool, then wrap the ribbon around from both sides and tie in a bow.

COME TOGETHER

Gather all of your favorite people for a party with a

retro flair. Whether you're throwing a high-style cocktail

party or a comfort-food luncheon, you'll find the perfect

invitation and decorations in

this section. It's easy to adapt the

pieces to fit your own special

occasion with a simple change in

wording or paper selection. C'mon,

let's get this party rolling!

You are invited
Hedda...

Dear Chicks and...
bu...

Murder Mystery Dinner

Tragical Mystery Tour

March 19, 2005

Kamber

"Tragical Mystery Tour"
HOST-A-MURDER DINNER
March 19, 2005

MARTINI TIME
INVITATION
Alison Eads

ALL i NEED

DOTS SCRAPBOOK
PAPER (DOODLEBUG
DESIGNS)

SILVER METALLIC
PAPER

GLITTER CONFETTI
VELLUM

SABLE METALLIC SWIRL
CARDSTOCK (PAPER
ADVENTURES)

LIGHT PINK
CARDSTOCK

COCKTAIL STICKERS
(MEMORY SHOPPE)

SCISSORS

GLUE STICK

RULER

FONT: NEW YORKER

PLEASE JOIN US FOR
COCKTAILS
(AND MOCKTAILS)
FEBRUARY 14, 2005
8:00PM

(BLACK TIE OPTIONAL)

MARTINI TIME!

Watching the Thin Man movies from the 1940s (with Myrna Loy and William Powell) inspired this somewhat glamorous party idea. Since the martini is back in vogue, wouldn't it be fun to invite some friends over to enjoy a few old-fashioned cocktails?

1 Cut a piece of sable cardstock and a piece of the dots paper to 5¼" x 11" (13cm x 28cm). Glue the wrong sides together using glue stick.

2 Place the card horizontally on your work surface with the black side down. Score a line at 3¼" (8cm) and at 7½" (19cm) from the left side. Using scissors, cut a scalloped edge on the left edge.

3 Fold the piece up so that the dotted paper is on the inside. Print the party information on pink cardstock, trim to approximately 3½" x 4½" (9cm x 11cm) and use glue stick to adhere to the center panel on the inside of the folded invitation.

4 Print row after row of cocktail names (repeating) onto the vellum. Place the card horizontally on the work surface with the dot side down. Trim the vellum and a second piece of dot paper to the size of the right hand panel (the side with the straight edge). Layer the vellum on the dots and the dots on the right panel of the card using glue stick.

5 Create a band that is 8" (20cm) long to go around the invitation with layers of the following three papers: pink cardstock 1⅞" (5cm) wide, silver metallic paper 1⅝" (4cm) wide, and the dot paper 1" (3cm) wide. Print "Martini Time!" onto vellum and cut this as the top layer for the strip, trimming to about ¾" (2cm) wide.

6 Glue the strips together with craft glue or glue stick. Wrap them snugly around the invitation, then glue the ends of the strip to secure. Embellish the bottom right corner of the folded invitation with a cocktail sticker to finish.

These glass charms are a natural for carrying the martini theme into the décor for your party.

Pretty beads and vellum add to the glamour of the evening.

MARTINI TiME
GLASS CHARMS
Alison Eads

ALL i NEED

DOTS SCRAPBOOK PAPER (DOODLEBUG DESIGNS)

SABLE METALLIC SWIRL CARDSTOCK (PAPER ADVENTURES)

GLITTER CONFETTI VELLUM

METAL RIMMED CIRCLE TAGS

SILVER HOOP EARRING WIRES

ASSORTED BEADS

HEAD PINS

ROUND-NOSED PLIERS

CIRCLE PAPER PUNCH

1/8" (3MM) HOLE PUNCH

SCISSORS

GLUE STICK

FONT: NEW YORKER

1 Thread three or four beads onto a head pin. Using the round-nosed pliers, create a loop at the end of the pin. Hang the beaded dangle from an earring wire. Repeat for the remaining number of charms.

2 Punch or cut circles from the sable and dot papers and, using glue stick, adhere to both sides of the metal rimmed tags. Feel for the hole in the tag and repunch the papers with the ⅛" (3mm) hole punch.

3 Print cocktail names on the vellum. Punch circles around the names and glue to the tags, with some of the circle extending off of the tag. Trim the vellum to the edge of the tag with scissors. Thread the tags onto the earring wires to finish.

TRAGICAL MYSTERY TOUR INVITATION

Laurie Dewberry

ALL I NEED

SCRAPBOOK CARDSTOCK:
- FLASHY FLOWERS (SEI)
- SHOWY STREAKS STRIPES (SEI)
- LOVE BEADS DOTS (SEI)
- GO-GO GREEN SOLID CARDSTOCK (SEI)

WHITE CARDSTOCK

FRAMES, TABS AND LABELS SHEET, HIPPIE CHICK (SEI)

DOUBLE-SIDED TAPE

CRAFT GLUE

WHITE, SQUARE ENVELOPE

FONT: BELLBOTTOM

This invitation was created for a murder mystery dinner party with a hippie theme. Opening this groovy invitation will transport your guests back to the 1960s and set the stage for a far-out party!

1 Trim a piece of the stripes paper to 11" x 5½" (28cm x 14cm) and fold in half to 5½" (14cm) square.

2 Print the name of your event on white cardstock and cut down to an oval shape. Here, I used a green printed border around the text and included a few retro flowers. Cut a ¼" (6mm) slit in the top and bottom of the oval.

3 Cut a strip from the dots paper, following the contour of the dots. Slide the strip of paper through the slits in the oval cutout and wrap around the front of the folded cardstock. Affix to the inside with a dab of glue on each end.

4 Trim a 1½" (4cm) strip of the flowers paper to create a pocket for the party information. Adhere it to the bottom inside of the folded cardstock by applying a line of double-sided tape to it along the bottom. Crease the strip along the fold of the card.

5 Print the invitation information on 5" (13cm) squares of white and green cardstock.

6 Add a tab to the top of the invitation and a flower label to the flap on the white envelope, selecting from those on the coordinating label and tag paper.

This piece doubles as a place marker for the dinner and a keepsake frame for each guest. For the party, hang the frames from the backs of the chairs with each guest's name inside. Send the frame home with each guest so they can place a party photo inside.

TRAGICAL MYSTERY TOUR PLACE CARD

Laurie Dewberry

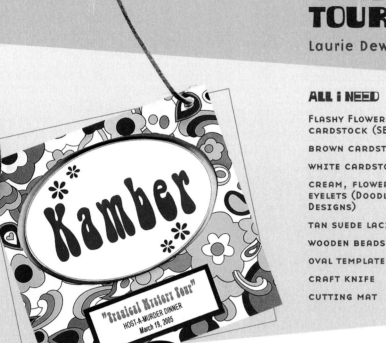

ALL i NEED

FLASHY FLOWERS CARDSTOCK (SEI)

BROWN CARDSTOCK (SEI)

WHITE CARDSTOCK

CREAM, FLOWER-SHAPED EYELETS (DOODLEBUG DESIGNS)

TAN SUEDE LACING

WOODEN BEADS

OVAL TEMPLATE

CRAFT KNIFE

CUTTING MAT

1/8" (3MM) HOLE PUNCH

EYELET SETTING TOOL

HAMMER

DIMENSIONAL ADHESIVE DOTS

DOUBLE-SIDED TAPE

FONT: BELLBOTTOM

1 Cut a 12" x 6" (30cm x 15cm) piece of the flowers paper and fold down to 6" (15cm) square.

2 Open up the paper and on one half, about ½" (1cm) from the fold and centered side to side, trace a 5" x 3½" (13cm x 9cm) oval using a template. With the paper open and on a cutting mat, cut out and remove the oval, using a craft knife.

3 Fold the place card closed and punch a hole just below the fold line on both ends of the card. Set the flower eyelets by inserting an eyelet through the front of the card and placing it face down on the cutting mat. Use the eyelet setter and a hammer to set the eyelets. (See page 89 for instructions.)

4 Print the guest's name on a piece of white cardstock. Here, I added a few retro flowers too. Trim the name using a 4¾" x 3¼" (12cm x 8cm) oval template. Apply dimensional adhesive dots to the back of the name piece. Center the name inside the cutout oval and adhere to the back inside panel of the card.

5 Print the event information on white cardstock and cut down to 3" x 1" (8cm x 3cm). Adhere the label to a piece of brown cardstock, using double-sided tape and trim down, leaving ⅛" (3mm) on all sides. Adhere the label to the front of the frame, using double-sided tape and center it below the oval.

6 String four beads on the suede lacing and string one end through each eyelet from the front to the back. Tie a knot at each end.

TROPiCAL INVITATION

Judi Watanabe

ALL i NEED

WHITE CARDSTOCK

VELLUM

HAWAIIAN PRINT
STAMP (JUDIKINS)

COCONUT PALM STAMP
(JUDIKINS)

TIKI IDOLS STAMP
(JUDIKINS)

RETRO INVITATION
STAMP (JUDIKINS)

SAND INK PAD

BROWN INK PAD

PINK INK PAD

BLACK INK PAD

DOUBLE-SIDED TAPE

Cocktail and dinner parties were super popular in the 1950s, so when tropical motifs became the rage after Hawaii became a state, tropical-themed dinner parties only made sense. Pick your own excuse for having a tropical party and enjoy!

1 Trim a piece of white cardstock to 5½" x 4¼" (14cm x 11cm). Smear pink ink directly from the ink pad onto the two long sides of the white cardstock, keeping the ink within 1" (3cm) of the edge. Stamp the Hawaiian print stamp in brown ink, over the pink areas, running the stamp off of the three edges. The print should not extend past the pink areas.

2 Stamp the Tiki idol stamp in brown ink on the left side of the card, centered between the two Hawaiian print borders. Stamp the palm tree three times with sand ink across the remaining white area of the cardstock.

3 Stamp the invitation stamp onto the piece of vellum with black ink. Line the vellum up on the stamped card so that there's a ½" (1cm) overhang at the top of the card and the party information text falls on top of the area stamped by palm trees. Cut the vellum to fit. Fold the overhang to the back of the card and adhere with double-sided tape.

Need some simple decorations for the drink table at your tropical bash? These drink stirrers are fun and funky and will have your noncrafty friends wondering how you made them.

TROPICAL
DRINK STIRRERS
Judi Watanabe

ALL i NEED

TRANSPARENT SHRINK PLASTIC

TIKI IDOLS STAMP (JUDIKINS)

PINEAPPLE STAMP (JUDIKINS)

HAWAIIAN CUBE #1 STAMP FOR ISLAND DANCER AND FLOWER IMAGES (JUDIKINS)

RICKY TICKY STICKIES CUBE STAMP (JUDIKINS)

PEACH CHALK INK PAD

OLIVE CHALK INK PAD

YELLOW-GREEN INK PAD

BROWN INK PAD

SCISSORS

BAKING PARCHMENT

COOKIE SHEET

1 Stamp a row of pineapples onto the shrink plastic, inking the leaf portion of the image with olive ink and alternate the pineapple portion with brown and peach inks. Stamp six images, and then stamp a Tiki idol image at the top of the row in brown ink.

2 Stamp three more rows of images, using the island dancer and floral stamps. Smear a section of the plastic with yellow-green ink and then stamp the dancer in a row on top of it. Stamp two of the floral images in one row (alternating color between olive and peach) and the other two floral images in another row (alternating color again). Stamp a different Tiki idol image at the top of each row.

3 After the images are completely dry, cut around them with scissors. Place the plastic on baking parchment on a cookie sheet, and bake at 300°F (150°C) for a few minutes until the plastic has shrunk and flattened out. Remove from the oven and, while they are still warm, press flat with the flat side of a large wood-mounted stamp or similar object.

MOM'S DINER
INVITATION

Alison Eads

ALL I NEED

Debossed Daisy cardstock paper (SEI)

Double-sided scrapbook cardstock:
- Tea Towel/ Kitchen Tiles (SEI)
- Housecoat/ Dainty Dots (SEI)

Brown cardstock

White cardstock

Turquoise cardstock

Granny's Tags set (SEI)

Brown gingham ribbon

Color-coordinated striped grosgrain ribbon

Scissors

Glue stick

Craft glue

Fonts: Beauty School Dropout, Dyspepsia, Dymaxion Script

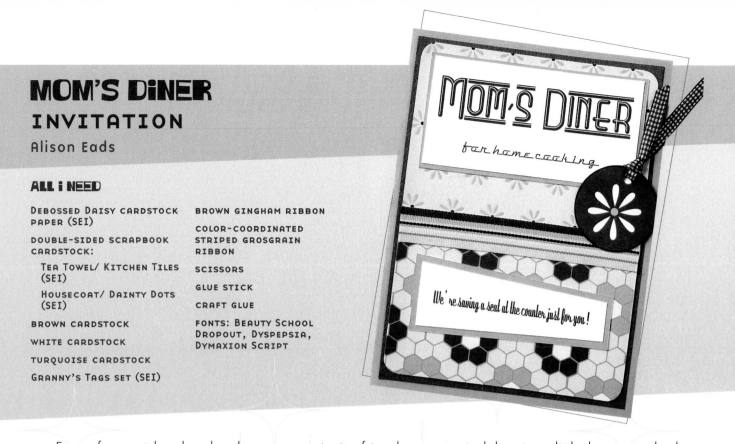

For a fun, yet low-key luncheon party, invite friends over to indulge in a little home-cooked nostalgia. Serve up a classic mom-type dinner, diner style. Turn on those *Leave it to Beaver* reruns and let everyone be a kid again. Yes, blowing bubbles in your milk is allowed!

1 Print the text for the top portion of the invitation onto white cardstock, using a brown color for the text. Trim the text to 2" x 4" (5cm x 10cm). Print "We're saving a seat at the counter just for you!" in a brown text color. Trim to a retro rectangle that is wider on the left side than it is on the right.

2 Layer the white cardstock text pieces onto turquoise cardstock and trim each piece, leaving a ⅛" (3mm) turquoise border.

3 Fold a piece of 10" x 6½" (25cm x 17cm) turquoise cardstock into a 5" x 6½" (13cm x 17cm) card. Trim a piece of brown cardstock to 4⅝" x 6⅛" (12cm x 16cm), and using glue stick, adhere it to the front of the card, centering it in both directions. Trim a piece of Debossed Daisy paper to 4½" x 6" (11cm x 15cm) and round the corners with scissors or a corner rounder punch. Layer this onto the center of the brown cardstock. Trim a piece of Kitchen Tile paper to 4½" x 2½" (11cm x 6cm), round two corners on a 4½" (11cm) side and layer that to the bottom of the previous paper.

4 Glue a 4½" (11cm) length of the striped grosgrain ribbon over the seam of the two patterned papers, using craft glue.

5 Using glue stick, layer the "Mom's Diner" text at the top portion of the card and the smaller text piece to the lower portion of the card. Tie a round tag with a piece of brown gingham ribbon, and glue the tag to the right, center area of the card, overlapping the striped ribbon a bit.

6 For the inside of the invitation, print the information text in a brown ink color onto white cardstock. Trim to size and round the corners. Cut a piece of Housecoat paper to fit the back half of the inside of the card, and adhere it to the card with glue stick. Layer the text piece onto the patterned paper with more glue stick.

What says "diner" more than a cup of coffee? Wrap your favorite cup of joe in this cute cup cozy, and keep those bothersome glass rings at bay with coordinated coasters.

MOM'S DINER
COASTERS & CUP COZY

Alison Eads

DOUBLE-SIDED
SCRAPBOOK
CARDSTOCK:
   Apron/ Table
   Ticking (SEI)
   Housecoat/ Dainty
   Dots (SEI)
   Tea Towel/
   Kitchen Tiles (SEI)

WHITE CARDSTOCK

BROWN CARDSTOCK

TURQUOISE ACRYLIC
PAINT

3 1/2" (9CM) WOODEN
DISCS, 4

CORK SHEET

PAINTBRUSH

PENCIL

SCISSORS

CRAFT KNIFE

CUTTING MAT

ACRYLIC SEALER

CRAFT GLUE

PATTERN ON PAGE 90

FONTS: BEAUTY
SCHOOL DROPOUT,
DYMAXION

CUP COZY

1 Trace the pattern (or use a cozy from your favorite coffee shop as a template) onto one of the double-sided papers. Cut the shape out with scissors.

2 Print the text for the cozy onto white cardstock using a brown text color. Here, I wrote "Mom's Diner" and "for home cooking". Trim the text to 1¾" x 4" (4cm x 10cm).

3 Trim a piece of brown cardstock to 2" x 4¼" (5cm x 11cm) and center the text piece onto the brown cardstock, adhering with craft glue. Using more glue, place the layered piece on the center of the cozy.

4 Glue the edges of the cozy together and slip around a cup or glass. Repeat for the other cozies.

COASTERS

1 Paint the wooden discs with the turquoise paint and allow to dry.

2 Place one disc on a sheet of paper and trace it with a pencil. Use scissors to cut out the circle just a bit smaller than the traced line. Repeat for the other coasters using different papers. Brush clear acrylic sealer onto the four discs and adhere the papers. Brush additional sealer over the papers and onto the edges of the discs. Set aside to dry.

3 Using craft glue, adhere the discs to the cork sheet. When they are dry, place on a cutting mat and trim around the edges with a craft knife.

MOM'S DiNER
NAPKIN RINGS &
STRAW HOLDER
Alison Eads

ALL i NEED

DOUBLE-SIDED
SCRAPBOOK CARDSTOCK:

APRON/ TABLE TICKING
(SEI)

HOUSECOAT/ DAISY
DOTS (SEI)

TEA TOWEL/ KITCHEN
TILES (SEI)

BROWN CARDSTOCK

WHITE CARDSTOCK

GRANNY'S TAG SET (SEI)

BROWN GINGHAM RIBBON

SCISSORS

1/4" (6MM) HOLE PUNCH

GLUE STICK

CRAFT GLUE

FONTS: DYSPEPSIA

Bring back memories of your favorite
"Mom" sayings by incorporating them into
these snazzy napkin rings and straw holders.
And don't forget to eat your peas!

NAPKIN RINGS

1 Cut a 1½" x 5" (4cm x 13cm) strip from one of the patterned cardstocks. Cut a coordinating, but different paper strip that is ½" x 5" (1cm x 13cm). Form the larger strip into a circle, overlapping the edges about ½" (1cm). Secure the ends with craft glue. Glue the smaller strip around the center of the circle and secure with more craft glue. Repeat this process for three additional napkin rings, varying the papers used.

2 Using the ¼" (6mm) hole punch, punch a hole near the outside edge of each ring.

3 Print witty sayings on white cardstock, using a brown text color. Phrases should be things mom used to say like: "Did you wash your hands?", "It's your favorite!", "Eat your peas!", or "Just one more bite!"

4 Trim the phrases to retro rectangle shapes, layer onto brown or turquoise cardstock, and trim to leave an ⅛" (3mm) border. Layer the phrases onto tags from the coordinating tag set using glue stick.

5 Tie the tags onto the napkin rings with pieces of gingham ribbon.

STRAW HOLDER

1 In a brown text color, print "Blow Bubbles in your Milk" onto white cardstock. (See photo for line breaks.) Trim the text down to a retro rectangle shape that is wider at the top than at the bottom. The piece here is 2⅜" (6cm) high, 1¼" (3cm) wide at the top and ¾" (2cm) wide at the bottom.

2 Layer the trimmed white piece onto brown cardstock and trim leaving an ⅛" (3mm) brown border.

3 Trim a piece of double-sided cardstock to 1¾" x 3⅞" (4cm x 10cm) and round the corners using scissors or a corner rounder punch. Layer the text piece onto the patterned paper piece, using craft glue. Punch a hole for the straw at each end of the piece using the ¼" (6mm) hole punch.

The space race was moving quickly during the 1950s and 60s and atoms, rockets and martians were a hot topic of style at atomic-themed dinner parties. Using shrink plastic and this rocket stamp, make an entire series of drink stirrers and cute decorations for the table.

ROCKiN' ROCKET
COCKTAIL STIRRERS
Judi Watanabe

ALL i NEED

TRANSPARENT SHRINK PLASTIC

ASTRO ROCKET STAMP (JUDIKINS)

BLACK PERMANENT INK

COLORED PENCILS

SCISSORS

RULER

PENCIL

CRAFT KNIFE

CUTTING MAT

BAKING PARCHMENT

COOKIE SHEET

1 Along the top edge of a sheet of transparent shrink plastic, stamp the rocket three times using the black ink. Stamp the image so that it is pointing up slightly. Trim the shrink plastic sheet 4½" (11cm) from the bottom of the rocket images.

2 After the black ink has dried, color in the rockets with colored pencils. From the underside of each rocket, draw two parallel lines with the ruler from the rocket to the bottom of the sheet. Draw the lines ¼" (6mm) apart. With the shrink plastic sheet on a cutting mat, cut along the lines with a ruler and craft knife. Cut out the rocket portion of each with scissors.

3 Place the trimmed rockets onto a piece of baking parchment on a cookie sheet. Bake at 300°F (150°C) for a few minutes until the plastic has shrunk and flattened out. Remove from the oven and press the pieces while they are still warm with the flat side of a large wood-mounted stamp or similar flat object.

MY GUY
TABLE SIGN
Laurie Dewberry

ALL i NEED

SCRAPBOOK PAPERS:
  POP CIRCLES (KI MEMORIES)
  SIMPLE STRIPE (KI MEMORIES)
  CANTEEN GREEN CARDSTOCK (KI MEMORIES)
  LIGHT BLUE CARDSTOCK

WHITE CARDSTOCK
DOWEL ROD
WHITE ACRYLIC PAINT
PAINTBRUSH
GLUE STICK
FONTS:
  ARIAL
  DINER SCRIPT

Inspired by classic neon signs, this table decoration offers a unique alternative to a traditional birthday banner. Set in a drink tub on a buffet table or in a vase wrapped with paper, this sign is sure to delight the birthday guest of honor.

1 Print the letters to spell "Birthday" onto white cardstock. I used a large point size and broke the word after the *B* and the *h* so that it would fit on a standard piece of paper.

2 Cut out the letters and glue onto two pieces of Canteen paper that have been glued together. Trim the paper to a 5½ x 16¾" (14cm x 43cm) rectangle, then round the corners using scissors.

3 Glue the rectangle to two pieces of the stripe paper that have been glued together. Trim to leave ¼" (6mm) of the stripe paper on all sides.

4 In brown ink, print the word "Happy" surrounded by a parallelogram shape with rounded corners onto light blue cardstock. Trim leaving ⅛" (3mm) around the printed parallelogram line.

5 Print the name of the guest of honor surrounded by a rectangle border in brown ink on light blue cardstock. Glue the trimmed name to a piece of the circles paper, and trim leaving ⅜" (10mm) on all sides.

6 Glue the word "Happy" to the front, top left of the green cardstock and glue the name to the back of the bottom right of the sign.

7 Using white acrylic paint, paint a wooden dowel and, when dry, attach the dowel to the back of the sign using craft glue. To further secure, glue a strip of paper over the end of the dowel on the back of the sign.

The shape of this card and the paper and embellishments used give the look of a man's dress shirt from the 1960s. Slip the greeting into the pocket for a card your guy will love.

MY GUY
BIRTHDAY CARD
Laurie Dewberry

ALL i NEED

SCRAPBOOK PAPERS:
  POP CIRCLES (KI MEMORIES)
  CHIC STRIPE NARROW STRIPE (KI MEMORIES)
  WISDOM (KI MEMORIES)
CANTEEN GREEN CARDSTOCK
DIE-CUT LABELS AND EMBELLISHMENTS, MY GUY (KI MEMORIES)
ICE CANDY ACRYLIC EMBELLISHMENTS, MY GUY (KI MEMORIES)

NEEDLE
BROWN THREAD
LIGHT BLUE THREAD
BLUE BUTTON
SEWING MACHINE
SCISSORS
DOUBLE-SIDED TAPE
CRAFT GLUE
FONT: ARIAL

1 Print the words "Happy Birthday" on the green cardstock and trim to 7" x 3¾" (18cm x 9.5cm).

2 Glue a brown label holder to the top center of the card (so the window is in the back) with craft glue. Then glue a clear acrylic embellishment to the center of the label.

3 Cut an 8" x 8" (20cm x 20cm) piece of the narrow stripe paper and fold in half to 4" x 8" (10cm x 20cm), so the stripes are parallel to the fold. From the top of the card, cut on the fold for 2" (5cm), then cut horizontally across to remove a 2" x 4" (5cm x 10cm) section from the back side of the card.

4 Cut a 4" x 2½" (10cm x 6cm) piece of the circles paper. With wrong sides together, adhere it to the half of the stripe paper that is taller with double-sided tape. Fold the card back together. The shorter half of the stripe paper should be covering the bottom edge of the circles paper. Round all four corners with scissors or a corner rounder.

5 Using a sewing machine, with brown thread in the needle and light blue thread in the bobbin, sew around the sides and bottom (with the stripe paper side up) to create a pocket.

6 Fold down the top of the pocket, so that the circles paper is now visible and is sitting on top of the stripe paper. Sew a button in the center of the cutout, about two-thirds of the way down from the top, securing the portion that is folded down to the pocket.

7 Affix the "My Guy" cutout from the Wisdom paper to the bottom right of the pocket. Write your sentiments on the green card and stick it in the pocket.

GETTING CRAFTY
If you're sending the card in the mail, create an envelope to match. To make a template, carefully tear apart a plain envelope that fits the card and trace the shape onto coordinating paper.

GiRLY-GiRL
INVITATION
Alison Eads

ALL i NEED

DOUBLE-SIDED SCRAPBOOK
CARDSTOCK:

   LOVE MUFFIN DOTS/ LOVE BIRD
   BLUE (SEI)

   SWEET PEA PINK DOTS/
   SWEETHEART MEDIUM PINK
   (SEI)

WHITE CARDSTOCK

HOT STUFF DARK PINK
CARDSTOCK (SEI)

PINK MARKER

SCISSORS

GLUE STICK

CLIP ART IMAGE (SEE SIDEBAR
ON PAGE 47)

FONT: A&S SWAN

Did you know?

Patty is having a Party!
It's a girly-girl birthday party
January 26, 2005
7:00 pm until ?
Let's celebrate friendship
and everything that's great about being a girl.
Put on your twinsets and bobby socks,
tie your hair in a ponytail and get ready to play!

This party for grown-up girls
features a cashmere-sweater color scheme
and lots of monogrammed girly-girl goodies.
This invitation sets the tone of the party and
ensures a girls-only good time.

1 Print a clip art image along with "Did you know?" text onto white cardstock. Trim the printed piece to 3½" (9cm) square and use a pink marker or chalk ink pad to add color to the edge.

2 Trim a piece of dots paper to 4½" (11cm) square and, using glue stick, layer it onto the dark pink cardstock. Trim leaving ½" (1cm) on all sides. Center the printed piece and adhere to the layered squares using glue stick.

3 Print the party information onto pink dots paper. Trim to 4½" (11cm) square and adhere, using glue stick, to the blue side of a piece of double-sided cardstock. Trim, leaving ½" (1cm) of the blue on all sides. Glue the layered party info piece to the back of the layered clipart piece using glue stick.

Let these cute place cards help your friends find their seats and lead them to their personalized votive favors. These little votive holders, complete with pearl beaded monogram charms and filled with candles—or chocolate—will make your guests feel pampered!

GiRLY-GiRL PLACE CARD & VOTIVE FAVOR

Alison Eads

ALL i NEED

GLASS VOTIVE HOLDER

HONEY BUNCH BROWN DOTS/ LOVE BIRD BLUE DOUBLE-SIDED SCRAPBOOK CARDSTOCK (SEI)

CUTIE PIE PINK DOT CARDSTOCK (SEI)

SWEETHEART MEDIUM PINK CARDSTOCK (SEI)

SMALL PEARL BEADS

PINK SATIN RIBBON

24-GAUGE WIRE

JUMP RINGS

ROUND-NOSED PLIERS

CRAFT KNIFE

CUTTING MAT

CIRCLE PUNCH OR TEMPLATE

SCISSORS

SCALLOPED-EDGE SCISSORS (LARGE PATTERN)

GLUE STICK

CRAFT GLUE

FONT: A&S SWAN

PLACE CARD

1 Cut the brown dot paper to 3" x 4" (8cm x 10cm) and fold to make a 3" x 2" (8cm x 5cm) card.

2 Print the guest's name on medium pink paper. Cut a circle around the name, using a circle punch or template and scissors, leaving the text near the edge of the circle rather than in the center.

3 Glue the circle to the front of the card, with part of the circle overhanging the edge. Trim the excess circle with scissors.

VOTIVE HOLDER

1 Cut the pink dot paper to fit around the glass votive holder with about ½" (1cm) of overlap. Secure around the holder with craft glue.

2 Cut a brown dot strip of paper and trim one long edge with the scalloped-edge scissors. Glue this around the holder at the top.

3 Cut a length of wire and, using round-nosed pliers, create a tiny loop at one end. Thread pearl beads onto the wire and bend into initials. Trim the wire, leaving 1" (3cm) extra at the end. Make a second tiny loop at this end and trim the excess. Add a jump ring to the top loop of the initial. Cut a length of pink satin ribbon, thread the jump ring on the ribbon, and tie the beaded initial near the top of the votive holder.

GIRLY-GIRL PURSE FAVOR & DIARY

Alison Eads

ALL I NEED

- SMALL COMPOSITION BOOK
- DOUBLE-SIDED SCRAPBOOK CARDSTOCK:
  - HONEY BUNCH BROWN DOTS/ LOVE BIRD BLUE (SEI)
  - SUGAR DADDY WIDE STRIPES/ PRINCESS LIGHT PINK (SEI)
  - CUTIE PIE PINK DOT CARDSTOCK (SEI)
  - HOT STUFF DARK PINK CARDSTOCK (SEI)

- NARROW PINK STRIPE CARDSTOCK(SEI)
- JUMBO MONOGRAM STICKERS (AMERICAN CRAFTS)
- PINK GROSGRAIN RIBBON
- PINK SATIN RIBBON
- WOOD (OR CHIPBOARD) TAG
- METAL-RIMMED TAG
- SMALL PEARL BEADS
- KEY CHARM (JOLEE'S)
- 24-GAUGE WIRE

- BALL CHAIN
- AQUA ACRYLIC PAINT
- PAINTBRUSH
- CRAFT KNIFE
- CUTTING MAT
- SCISSORS
- SCALLOPED-EDGE SCISSORS (SMALL PATTERN)
- 1/8" (3MM) HOLE PUNCH
- CIRCLE PUNCH OR TEMPLATE
- BONE FOLDER

- RULER
- GLUE STICK
- CRAFT GLUE
- MASKING TAPE
- HOOK AND LOOP FASTENER DOTS
- PURSE TEMPLATE (PAGE 91)
- FONT: A&S SWAN

Your guests will love this little paper purse that couldn't be more girly-girl. Fill it with lip gloss and nail polish in their favorite shades or with mints and gum, and let the party begin! And before the girls leave, give them each a monogrammed diary for all their secret thoughts.

PURSE

1 Using the pattern, cut out the purse shape from the pink dots paper. Fold along all the dashed lines by first scoring with a bone folder and a ruler.

2 Glue the side flaps to the front sides of the purse using craft glue.

3 Thread pearl beads on a length of wire long enough for a handle. Leave about 1" (3cm) of wire on either end unbeaded. Punch two holes at the top of the purse flap, about ½" (1cm) from the outside edges. Insert the ends of the wire into the holes and bend the ends. Secure the wire with masking tape on the inside of the purse. Cut a strip of coordinating paper and glue it over the taped wire.

4 Cut a large circle from blue cardstock and glue it to the front flap of the purse. Adhere a hook and loop fastener dot to the flap of the purse to keep it closed. Tie a pink grosgrain bow to the handle.

5 Paint the wooden tag with the aqua acrylic paint, using the paintbrush. Let it dry, then glue a piece of wide stripe paper to one side of the tag. Trim the excess paper with a craft knife on a cutting mat.

6 On the dark pink paper, print the guest's name. Cut a circle around the name, with the name off to one edge rather than centered. Adhere the circle to the paper side of the tag, using craft glue, with the circle extending over two sides of the tag in the top left corner. Trim the excess circle with scissors. Thread a ball chain through the tag and attach it in one of the handle holes.

SECRET DIARY

1 Glue the pink stripes paper to the front of the small composition book, using glue stick and leaving the spine uncovered. Open up the cover and with the inside of the cover face up, trim the excess paper with the craft knife, working on a cutting mat.

2 Layer strips of coordinating paper horizontally across the cover using glue stick. Trim the wider strip with the small scalloped-edge scissors.

3 Add a monogram sticker to the bottom right corner.

4 Print "for Secrets" onto pink dots paper and trim to fit the metal rimmed tag. Glue the circle onto the tag.

5 Tie the tag and a key charm onto the cover with pink satin ribbon. Wrap the ribbon around the front cover, tie at the top and push toward the spine.

MEMORIES ARE MADE OF THIS

There's no craftier way to preserve your precious

memories than with scrapbook pages. In this section

you'll find hip and happy pages that show off your

photos, whether they're new or old. Honor the guy in

your life with the Mellow Guy scrapbook page or

remember a fabulous evening

of fun with the Fifties Night

pages. Retro papers and

embellishments will make

your pages swing!

HOT DISH
SCRAPBOOK PAGE

Alison Eads

ALL I NEED

SCRAPBOOK PAPERS:
   STRAWBERRY (LEISURE ARTS)
   AQUA DOTS (MEMORIES IN THE MAKING)
   RED FLOWERS (KAREN FOSTER DESIGN)
   BLACK GINGHAM (THE PAPER PATCH)

RIBBED AQUA CARDSTOCK

WHITE CARDSTOCK

1950S COOKING IMAGES (PAPER REFLECTIONS)

PAGES FROM AN OLD COOKBOOK

EMBROIDERED HEARTS RIBBON

BLACK SATIN RIBBON

BLACK EMBROIDERY FLOSS

ASSORTED BUTTONS

SILVERWARE CHARMS (JOLEE'S)

FOAM ALPHABET STAMP (MAKING MEMORIES)

METAL RIMMED CIRCLE TAGS, 1 LARGE, 2 SMALL

MINI KRAFT PAPER BAG

RED INK PAD

SCISSORS

POSTAGE STAMP-EDGED SCISSORS

GLUE STICK

CRAFT GLUE

I've always loved to cook, and it all started with a cookbook for kids that I got a long time ago. These colors totally make me think of kitschy kitchen décor, and inspire a fun layout that celebrates preparing your favorite recipe.

1 Layer the four scrapbook papers over the ribbed aqua cardstock, adhering each piece with glue stick. Refer to the photo for layout suggestions.

2 Cut circles out of old cookbook pages to fit the metal rimmed tags. Adhere the circles to the tags with glue stick. Stamp an initial on the large tag, using the red ink pad and the foam alphabet stamp. Decorate the tags with buttons (thread black embroidery floss through the holes first), vintage images, ribbon and charms. Using craft glue, adhere the tags to the page. See photo for placement.

3 Trim one vintage image to fit within a frame of black squares on the black gingham paper. My image here was trimmed to 1¾" x 2¾" (4cm x 7cm). Adhere the image to the gingham paper and trim along the outside of the black checks "frame."

4 Using glue stick, glue the layered vintage image to the front of the mini kraft bag. Using craft glue, adhere a strip of the embroidered hearts ribbon diagonally across one corner. Fold the ends around to the back and secure with more glue. Glue the bag to the page.

5 Print your journaling on white cardstock, keeping your text blocks about 3½" x 1¼" (9cm x 3cm), numbering the pages to keep them in order. Trim the text blocks down to individual cards that are 2⁵⁄₁₆" x 4³⁄₁₆" (6cm x 11cm). Slide the stack of cards into the kraft bag.

6 Layer a photo on a full cookbook page and adhere to the page, using glue stick.

Good toys never go out of style. And that's true for this pull toy that has been rediscovered by a new generation of kids. Taking a quick picture of just one of the duckies gave me the perfect finishing touch for this page.

FAVORITE TOY
SCRAPBOOK PAGE
Christine Doyle

ALL I NEED

BE BOP SWIZZLESTICKS SCRAPBOOK PAPER (SEI)

GREEN CARDSTOCK

LIGHT BLUE CARDSTOCK

RED CARDSTOCK

WHITE CARDSTOCK

BE BOP CARDSTOCK ALPHABET STICKERS (SEI)

BROWN INK PAD

SCISSORS

RULER

DOUBLE-SIDED TAPE

DIMENSIONAL ADHESIVE DOTS

FONT: AMERICAN TYPEWRITER

1 Cut a piece of green cardstock to 11" x 2½" (28cm x 6cm). Tap the edges in brown ink and tape this piece to the top of the scrapbook paper with double-sided tape.

2 Cut 1" (3cm) squares from red cardstock, one for each letter in your headline. Remove the letter stickers and center one on each square. Cut 1½" (4cm) circles from light blue cardstock and layer the squares onto the circles with double-sided tape.

3 Tape the circles onto the long green cardstock, using double-sided tape on some circles and dimensional adhesive dots on others. Here I staggered the letters to make them look like a row of ducks.

4 Trim a photo to size, then use double-sided tape to adhere to a piece of white cardstock. Trim the cardstock to leave a ¼" (6mm) border on the sides and ⅛" (3mm) on the top and bottom.

5 Cut a piece of green cardstock about 1" (3cm) wider and longer than the layered photo. Tap the edges of the green cardstock in brown ink. Use double-sided tape to adhere the layered photo at an angle on the green cardstock, then tape the piece to the scrapbook page.

6 Print your journaling onto white cardstock and cut it into a retro shape that's wider at one end. Adhere the cardstock to the page with double-sided tape. Carefully cut out a toy image and adhere it under the journaling with double-sided tape.

PRINCE CHARMING
SCRAPBOOK PAGE
Judi Watanabe

ALL i NEED

RECORDS SCRAPBOOK PAPER
(KAREN FOSTER DESIGN)

STARS VELLUM (SEI)

CLEAR VELLUM

IVORY CARDSTOCK

ENGAGEMENT STAMP
(JUDIKINS)

CHARM BRACELET

BLACK GROSGRAIN RIBBON

BLACK INK PAD

LARGE NEEDLE

3" (8CM) CIRCLE PUNCH

DECKLE-EDGED SCISSORS

DOUBLE-SIDED TAPE

GLUE STICK

I knew I would find my Prince Charming. Who would have guessed he was just around the corner?

Every high school girl's dream during the middle of the century was to marry Prince Charming and live happily ever after. The paper printed with 45 rpm records makes a great setting for photos depicting a teenager's life.

1 Adhere stars vellum to the records paper, using double-sided tape. Try to place the tape in areas where the photos will cover it up.

2 Layer photos onto ivory cardstock, using glue stick, and trim each one with the deckle-edged scissors to leave about ⅛" (3mm) of the cardstock showing around the sides of each photo.

3 Print your journaling onto ivory cardstock and trim with the deckle-edged scissors to a rectangle about 4½" x 1¾" (11cm x 4cm).

4 Adhere the layered photos to the vellum, using double-sided tape. Three smaller photos on the left and one larger photo on the right make a nice composition.

5 Trim a piece of the ribbon to about 7" (18cm). To attach the charm bracelet to the edge of the ribbon, make small holes with a needle about ¾" (2cm) in from each end. Put the clasp through one hole and the jump ring on the opposite end through the other hole.

6 Position the ribbon about 1" (3cm) from the bottom of the larger photo, centering the bracelet (see photo for reference). Adhere the ribbon to the vellum using double-sided tape, tucking the left end under the bottom photo. Adhere the trimmed journaling over the ribbon with more tape.

7 Using black ink, stamp the engagement stamp onto the clear vellum. When the ink has dried, punch the image out with a 3" (8cm) circle punch. Place a couple of small pieces of double-sided tape under the inked portions of the image and adhere the circle to the top right corner of the large photo to finish.

The only child at a party filled with doting adults always has to be in front of the camera and in the center of everything. The theme is timeless, but these 1960s inspired papers are a perfect match for the photos.

CRASHING THE PARTY
SCRAPBOOK PAGE
Judi Watanabe

ALL I NEED

SCRAPBOOK PAPERS:
   RECORDS (KAREN FOSTER DESIGN)
   DYNAMIC RETRO (COLORBOK)
RED CARDSTOCK
APPLE GREEN VELLUM, 8 1/2" X 11"
(22CM X 28CM)
CLEAR VELLUM
GOLD PHOTO CORNERS
SLIDE MOUNTS, 5
FINE-POINT BLACK PEN
CRAFT GLUE
DOUBLE-SIDED TAPE

1 Place a line of double-sided tape along one 8½" (22cm) edge of the green vellum. Adhere the vellum to the graphic print page, centered top to bottom and with the side opposite the taped edge flush against the left edge of the page.

2 Cut a strip of the records paper 3½" (9cm) wide. Using double-sided tape, layer it on the right side of the graphic print page, covering the taped side of the vellum.

3 Layer your photos onto red cardstock, using double-sided tape. Trim the cardstock down to leave about ⅛" (3mm) of the red cardstock showing on all sides. Place gold photo corners on each of the photos and, using double-sided tape, layer the photos onto the page (see photo for placement ideas).

4 Open up the slide mounts and place a trimmed piece of clear vellum inside each one. Close the mounts, gluing them closed with craft glue if necessary. Write your journaling on the vellum using a fine-point pen.

5 Adhere the journaled slide mounts to the page using craft glue, and arrange them so the journaling reads in the correct order.

MELLOW GUY SCRAPBOOK PAGE

Alison Eads

ALL i NEED

SCRAPBOOK PAPERS:
  STRIPE (7 GYPSIES)
  BLUE PAISLEY (CHATTERBOX)
  FLORAL (CHATTERBOX)
  RUSSET LINEN (CHATTERBOX)
  EARTHTONE PAISLEY (CREATIVE IMAGINATIONS)

DARK RUSSET BROWN CARDSTOCK
DARK GOLD CARDSTOCK
RUSSET INK PAD
ASSORTED BEADS
BEAD FLOSS
BEADING NEEDLE

T-PIN OR NEEDLE TOOL
SCISSORS
GLUE STICK
DOUBLE-SIDED TAPE
FONTS: BELLBOTTOM, PUPCAT

Although this photo was taken in the early 80s, the feel of it is definitely rooted in the 1970s. (Just look at those John Lennon glasses.) The gentle curves and paisleys on this layout epitomize a "go with the flow" vibe.

1 Begin with a 12" x 12" (30cm x 30cm) piece of dark russet brown cardstock as a foundation. Using scissors, trim strips of the scrapbook papers into gentle curves and waves. Create about five strips all together and layer them onto the outside edges of the page, using glue stick (refer to photo as a guide).

2 Repeat the wavy cutting for a large piece of the blue paisley to go in the middle of the smaller waves. Adhere to the page with glue stick. Glue your photo onto a piece of the earthtone paisley paper and trim to a shape that is straight on the sides and curved or slightly wavy on the top and bottom. Layer this onto the russet linen leaving ⅛" (3mm) of each color on the sides and top, but cut reverse wave lines at the bottom (see photo). Tap the edges of the linen paper onto the russet ink pad. Layer the linen paper onto dark gold cardstock. Leave ⅛" (3mm) of each color on the sides and top, but cut reverse wave lines at the bottom. Ink these edges on the russet ink pad as well.

3 Print the title for the page (here, "Mellow Guy") and your journaling onto dark gold cardstock. The title can be in the Bellbottom font, and the journaling in the Pupcat font. Trim both pieces down to appropriate sizes. Dip the edges of text pieces into the russet ink pad.

He's always been a very
Mellow Guy

Charlie in Grad School (1981)
THIS PHOTO CAPTURES THE ESSENCE OF MY DARLING
HUSBAND. YOUTHFUL-YET-WISE. PEACEFUL. CALM
AND INTELLIGENT. THAT'S CHARLIE. ALWAYS WAS.

4 Using a T-pin or needle tool, poke two holes into each dark gold cardstock piece, varying the distance between holes. Thread the needle with floss and insert the needle through the back of one piece to the front. Thread on several beads and insert the needle through the other hole from the front to the back. Tie the floss in the back and secure the floss with tape to the back of the cardstock. Repeat beading for the other two gold cardstock pieces.

5 Adhere the three pieces to the page. Place the photo and title in the blue paisley portion and the journaling at the bottom right.

MAKE iT RETRO

To set the stage for a retro-inspired scrapbook page, incorporate lyrics from a song from the time. With just a few lines from "That's Amore" or the musical Hair, you'll be able to set a tone that's perfect for your design.

DECADES OF FASHION SCRAPBOOK PAGES

Alison Eads

ALL i NEED

SCRAPBOOK PAPERS:

- POLKA DOTS (DELUXE DESIGNS)
- PINK SCRIPT (RUSTY PICKLE)
- BUCKLE (RUSTY PICKLE)
- PINK HARLEQUIN (PSX)
- RULERS (7 GYPSIES)

LIGHT PINK CARDSTOCK

BLACK CARDSTOCK

MINI PINK FILE FOLDER (RUSTY PICKLE)

FASHION CUT OUTS (BISOUS)

SCROLL RUBBER STAMP (RUBBER STAMPEDE)

CHARCOAL INK PAD

SQUARE METAL RIMMED TAG

CIRCLE METAL RIMMED TAG

PINK SAFETY PINS (MAKING MEMORIES)

ALPHABET TAG

EMBROIDERED ROSES RIBBON

ASSORTED VINTAGE BUTTONS

PINK RIBBON FLOWERS

DRESSMAKER'S PIN

SCISSORS

GLUE STICK

CRAFT GLUE

FONT: CRAWFORD

Pink and black just shouts 1950s to me: full skirts, fitted waists, hats, the whole bit. It seemed the perfect way to document my rather unorthodox fashion sense during my college years. This layout would work equally well for little girls playing dress-up, older girls getting ready for prom night, or any other event calling for high fashion!

1 Begin with two 12" x 12" (30cm x 30cm) light pink cardstock pages. Cut pieces of the pink script paper and polka dot paper and layer onto the pages, using glue stick. (See photo for approximate sizes and placement.) In opposite, upper corners, stamp the scroll image with the charcoal ink.

2 Mount photos onto black cardstock and trim, leaving ⅛" (3mm) of black on all sides. Adhere the layered photos to the pages, leaving the right side of the photo on the lefthand page adhesive-free so that you can later slide in the file folder.

3 Trim a buckle from the buckle print paper. Slip one 12" (30cm) length of embroidered ribbon through the buckle and adhere to the bottom of the left page using craft glue on the ribbon and glue stick on the buckle.

4 On one piece of the pink harlequin paper, print "A few Decades of Fashion" in the Crawford font and a 50s-era clip art image. Trim this piece and a plain pink harlequin piece to large tag shapes.

5 Layer the pink harlequin pieces onto black cardstock and trim, leaving ⅛" (3mm) of black on all sides. Embellish the tags with pieces from the ruler paper, buttons and flowers. At the top of each tag, glue a snippet of embroidered ribbon and attach a pink safety pin to each. Adhere the tags to the pages.

6 Print "Style Secrets" in the Crawford font at the top of the pink file folder. Journal on the inside of the folder. On the outside of the folder, layer fashion cutouts and a ruler piece, using glue stick to adhere. Embellish the folder with a ribbon flower and a piece of embroidered ribbon attached with a dressmaker's pin. Slide the folder behind the photo on the left page.

7 Embellish the metal rimmed tags with more buttons, ribbon and, if desired, printed paper. Adhere the tags and the alphabet tag to finish.

FIFTIES NIGHT
SCRAPBOOK PAGES
Laurie Dewberry

ALL i NEED

SCRAPBOOK PAPERS:

  NOSTALGIC DOTS AND STRIPES (RHONNA FARRER, AUTUMN LEAVES)

  DO THE POLKA DOTS (RHONNA FARRER, AUTUMN LEAVES)

WHITE CARDSTOCK

PINK CARDSTOCK

LETTER STICKERS, GROOVY GAL (SEI)

BLACK INK PEN

SCISSORS

DOUBLE-SIDED TAPE

GLUE STICK

This paper provides the perfect background for a 50s-themed scrapbook page. Keep your memories of twisting the night away for years to come with these playful pages.

1 Cut the three-stripes border from the dots and stripes paper and mount to the bottom of a plain dots sheet of paper, using double-sided tape. Repeat for the second page.

2 Adhere photos to white cardstock, using double-sided tape, then trim each to leave an 1/8" (3mm) border of white around each photo. Place on pages where desired, using more double-sided tape. Remember to leave room for title blocks.

3 Create title blocks by placing the stickers on white cardstock. Trim to funky retro shapes (see photo for ideas) and then adhere to pink cardstock, using glue stick. Trim each title piece to leave 3/16" (5mm) of pink on all sides.

4 Add retro stars with a black ink pen to one or both title blocks.

This reproduction of a classified advertisement is the perfect background for a 1940s style christening. Rickrack, that ever-popular embellishment for anything from dresses to dishtowels, gives this page a time stamp from mid-century.

CHRISTENING SCRAPBOOK PAGE

Judi Watanabe

ALL i NEED

DICTIONARY SCRAPBOOK PAPER (K&Company)

CREAM VELLUM

OFF WHITE CARDSTOCK

METALLIC BRONZE CARDSTOCK

COPPER-RIMMED TAG, 2" (5CM)

ORNATE HEART FRAME

SMALL COPPER FRAME CHARM

ANGEL CHARM

1/8" (3MM) COPPER EYELETS

1/16" (2MM) HOLE PUNCH

1/8" (3MM) HOLE PUNCH

2" (5CM) CIRCLE PUNCH

"CHERISH" RIBBON (ALL MY MEMORIES)

SABLE SILK RIBBON

SABLE RICKRACK

IVORY EMBROIDERY FLOSS OR FINE STRING

WALNUT INK

EYELET SETTING TOOL

HAMMER

PROTECTIVE MAT

BEIGE PAPER WASHERS

FOUNTAIN PEN

SMALL BRUSH

FINE-POINT BLACK PEN

RULER

DECKLE-EDGES SCISSORS

DOUBLE-SIDED TAPE

CRAFT GLUE

1 Trim pieces of vellum to about ¼" (6mm) larger each direction than the photos. Lay the vellum over the photos and decide which part of the photo you would like to "highlight." Use the circle punch to punch out a circle at those spots.

2 Using double-sided tape, layer the photos onto off-white cardstock and trim each to leave about ¼" (6mm) of cardstock showing on each side. Adhere the punched vellum pieces to the photos using small amounts of double-sided tape. Adhere the photos to the page with double-sided tape.

3 Attach a length of the silk ribbon and rickrack to the left side of the page, using small amounts of craft glue. Layer the "Cherish" ribbon onto the bronze cardstock, using double-sided tape, and trim it to leave ¼" (6mm) of the cardstock showing along both sides of the ribbon. Punch four holes using the ⅟₁₆" (2mm) hole punch at spots along the bottom of the cardstock where you will want to hang your tags and charms (see photo for reference). Adhere the layered ribbon to the center of the page, between the photographs, using double-sided tape.

4 With walnut ink and a fountain pen, write your journaling onto a piece of off-white cardstock. When dry, outline it with a fine-point black pen, using a ruler. Trim the journaling with deckle-edged scissors.

5 Using the ⅛" (3mm) hole punch, punch two holes at the side edges of the trimmed journaled piece. Insert an eyelet through a paper washer, and then into each hole. Set the eyelets on a protective surface, using the eyelet setting tool and a hammer. (See page 89 for instructions.)

6 Adhere the journaled piece to the top left corner of the page, using double-sided tape, placing it over the ribbon and rickrack.

7 Using a small brush, lightly dab small amounts of walnut ink onto the embroidery floss to age it. Set it aside to dry.

8 Trim photos to fit the copper tag, copper charm and heart frame. Use the aged embroidery floss to tie the embellishments to the punched holes in the metallic bronze cardstock.

SCHOOL DAYS SCRAPBOOK PAGE

Alison Eads

ALL I NEED

SCRAPBOOK PAPERS:
- YELLOW DAISY (KI MEMORIES)
- RED DOT (KI MEMORIES)
- STRIPE (KI MEMORIES)
- CHALKBOARD (KAREN FOSTER)

AVOCADO CARDSTOCK

RED CARDSTOCK

LIBRARY POCKET AND CARD (BOXER SCRAPBOOK PRODUCTIONS)

ALPHABET RUB-ONS (AUTUMN LEAVES)

EMBROIDERED RICKRACK

OLIVE BUTTONS, 3

PAGE FROM CHILDREN'S BOOK

SMALL ALPHABET STAMPS (HERO ARTS)

WALNUT INK

SMALL WOODEN RULER

SCISSORS

DAISY PUNCH (OPTIONAL)

GLUE STICK

CRAFT GLUE

STAPLER

FONT: ANTIQUE TYPE

For a 1970s twist on classic grade school colors, add a bit of gold and avocado. An illustration from that elementary school classic, *Dick and Jane*, decorates a library pocket that holds your journaling as well as a reduced copy of a child's school work.

1 Begin with a 12" x 12" (30cm x 30cm) piece of avocado cardstock as a foundation. Layer straight-edge strips of the scrapbook papers horizontally across the page as shown in the photo. Cut yellow daisy paper to be the largest strip. Center it, then surround it with narrower strips of the stripe. Lastly place chalkboard strips to the outside of the stripe. Leave about a 2" (5cm) strip of avocado at the bottom.

2 Cut a length of the embroidered rickrack the width of the page and, using craft glue, adhere it between the chalkboard and avocado at the bottom.

3 Cover the front of the library pocket with a page from a children's book. Using the alphabet stamps, stamp the year, teacher and school location on the front of the library card. Age the card a bit with walnut ink.

4 Make a reduced color copy of school work from the same year, and trim it to about 2¾" x 4" (7cm x 10cm). Adhere it to red cardstock and trim it to leave ⅛" (3mm) of red on all sides. Insert the library card and reduced artwork into the library pocket and glue to the right side of the page.

5 Adhere the photo to red cardstock using glue stick, and trim, leaving ³⁄₁₆" (5mm) on all sides. Round the corners with scissors or a corner rounder punch. Using glue stick, adhere the photo to the left side of the page. Write the age along the left side of the photo.

6 Print a very large grade number (200 pt. or so) onto avocado cardstock and trim closely. Use glue stick to glue the trimmed number to red cardstock and trim leaving ⅛" (3mm) of red on all sides. Adhere to the page, above the library card, using glue stick. Staple a snippet of the rickrack to the top right of the number.

7 Spell out the child's name on the ruler, using the rub-on letters. Stamp or rub on the grade also. Glue the ruler to the bottom of the page with craft glue.

8 Punch or cut out three daisies from the red dot paper and randomly glue them to the page. Using craft glue, add an olive button to the center of each flower for the final touch.

MAKE iT RETRO

Want to make your retro designs look like they're actually from the era? Try distressing some of the elements or adding a few stains.

To distress your paper or any embellishments, sand them lightly with sandpaper. To fade paper, set it out in the sun, and to age it, wipe it with walnut ink or dip it in a cup of tea. Coffee works well, too, for adding splatters or cup rings to your projects.

THE SUPPLIES YOU'LL NEED

Your path to fabulous retro paper projects will be smooth sailing when you have the right tools and know a few basic techniques.

Paper

The most important material in your projects is the paper. The paper you choose sets the mood for your project, and choosing the right weight of paper means your projects will be durable and easy to use. All of the following types of paper are found at craft, scrapbook and rubber stamp stores.

CARDSTOCK is a heavy-weight paper, often referred to as cover stock. It is available in solid colors, in both smooth and textured finishes, and with designs printed on either one side or both sides. Cardstock makes an excellent base for greeting cards, signs and folded boxes.

SCRAPBOOK OR DECORATIVE PAPERS are text-weight papers that have the feel of quality copier paper, but are printed on either one side or both sides. These papers are best used to decorate items that have more heft,

like containers or cardstock. A huge array of decorative papers is available.

VELLUM is a translucent paper that is layered over another paper to give it a unique look. Because vellum is translucent, tapes and glues will show through, so use adhesives sparingly or invest in ones created just for vellum.

Cutting Tools

Sure, a pair of scissors will handle all your cutting needs for these projects, but if you plan on creating a lot of paper projects, you may want to invest in some other cool tools to help you do the job.

A **CRAFT KNIFE**, like the X-acto brand knife, is great for making exact cuts in small areas. You can use it to trim around an image or to trim around an object that you've covered with

paper, like a coaster. Do your cutting on a cutting mat so that you don't damage your work surface.

A **PAPER TRIMMER**, available at craft and scrapbook stores, makes straight cuts a breeze. Whether you get one with a sliding blade or one with a swinging arm, you'll love how easy it is to use.

DECORATIVE SCISSORS work just like regular scissors but the blades create decorative edges when you cut. There is a wide variety of patterns available including deckle-edged, which looks like torn paper, and pinking shears.

Paper punches come in a variety of shapes and styles. There's the good ol' **HAND PUNCH** that you use to punch holes for eyelets and brads (see Embellishments on page 89), and an **ANYWHERE PUNCH** comes in handy for this same purpose. It's a tool with interchange-able metal heads that create different sized holes. To use the tool, place the head on paper then tap the end of the tool with a hammer to make the hole. Craft and scrapbook stores have **DECORATIVE PUNCHES** that come in lots of shapes and sizes, including large circles that work great for creating peepholes in cards.

Adhesives

The way you stick your projects together makes a big difference in how they'll hold up over time. Using the right adhesive for each job will keep your retro paper projects looking fresh for years to come.

DOUBLE-SIDED TAPE is a terrific all-purpose paper adhesive. Use it to affix decorative papers to cardstock or other items. When you use the acid-free, archival variety of double-stick tape, you don't need to worry about it damaging the paper over time.

GLUE STICK can be used in the same way as double-sided tape. The nice thing about glue stick is that you can easily (and more economically) give the item to be glued a solid covering of adhesive.

CRAFT GLUE, a general white tacky glue, is great for adhering heavier items like embellishments. By thinning craft glue with a little water, you can apply the glue with a brush for quick, solid coverage.

Stamping Supplies

Rubber stamp companies have been bitten by the retro bug and are coming out with lots of cool designs that will add a hip touch to your projects. With an ink pad and maybe a little embossing powder, you're good to go!

RUBBER STAMPS are available mounted to wooden blocks or unmounted. Either kind works just fine for the projects in this book, but for stamping on rounded surfaces, unmounted stamps work best.

PIGMENT INK PADS in any of a wide variety of colors contain a slow-drying ink that's perfect for use with embossing powders (see below). These inks work well on uncoated paper.

Other inks available include **SOLVENT INK**, also known as permanent ink, which works well on coated papers and any porous or nonporous surface. **DYE INKS** dry quickly and have the most vibrant color, but these colors will fade over time.

EMBOSSING POWDER comes in a variety of colors, including clear. It creates a dimensional effect when sprinkled on pigment ink and melted with a heat gun (also called an embossing gun, which blows air much hotter than a hair dryer). To heat emboss an image, stamp it on the surface using pigment ink. Sprinkle embossing powder on the ink while it's still wet, then tap the excess powder onto a sheet of scrap paper. Funnel the excess powder back into the container.

Use a paintbrush if necessary to wipe away any stray bits of powder from the surface. Heat the powder with the heat gun to melt, moving the gun continually so as not to burn the paper.

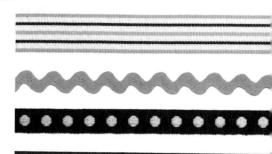

Embellishments

There's nothing like a little doodad or bit of texture to add a kick to any project. Embellishments like ribbon, charms, beads and stickers do just that. All of these are available at your local scrapbook, craft or rubber stamp store. Or stop by the fabric store and see what kind of goodies you can find there—maybe buttons and a little rickrack. A few favorite embellishments, eyelets and brads, may benefit from a little more explanation.

EYELETS are small metal grommets that you can use to secure papers on your projects or just to add interest. To secure an eyelet, punch a hole in your paper the size of the eyelet's shaft (usually $\frac{1}{16}$" or $\frac{1}{8}$" [2mm or 3mm]). Insert the shaft of the eyelet into the hole, and turn the paper over to the back side. Set your eyelet setting tool into the shaft and hit the end of the tool with a hammer to flare the shaft and secure the eyelet. Remove the setting tool, then hit the back of the eyelet itself with the hammer for good measure.

BRADS are metal embellishments that are backed with flanges to secure the brad to the paper. Punch a hole in the paper using the anywhere punch or the handheld punch. Insert the flanges of the brad into the hole and turn the paper to the back side. Press each flange down flat to the paper to secure.

PATTERNS

These patterns may be reproduced for the personal use of the reader.

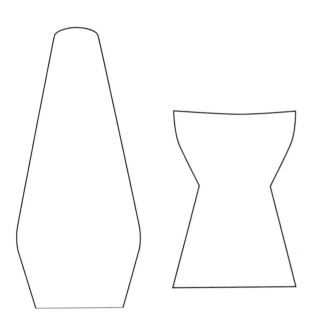

Thanks-A-Lava Card, page 27
Copy pattern at 100%.

Groovy Gal Card & Gift Can, pages 30, 31
Enlarge at 125% to bring to full size.

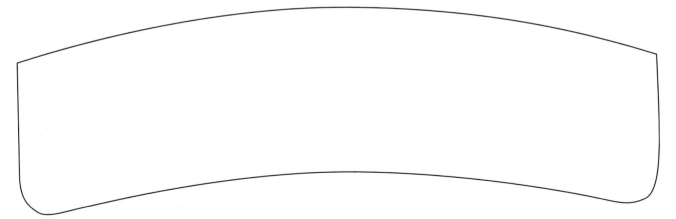

Mom's Diner Cup Cozy, page 65
Enlarge at 154% to bring to full size.

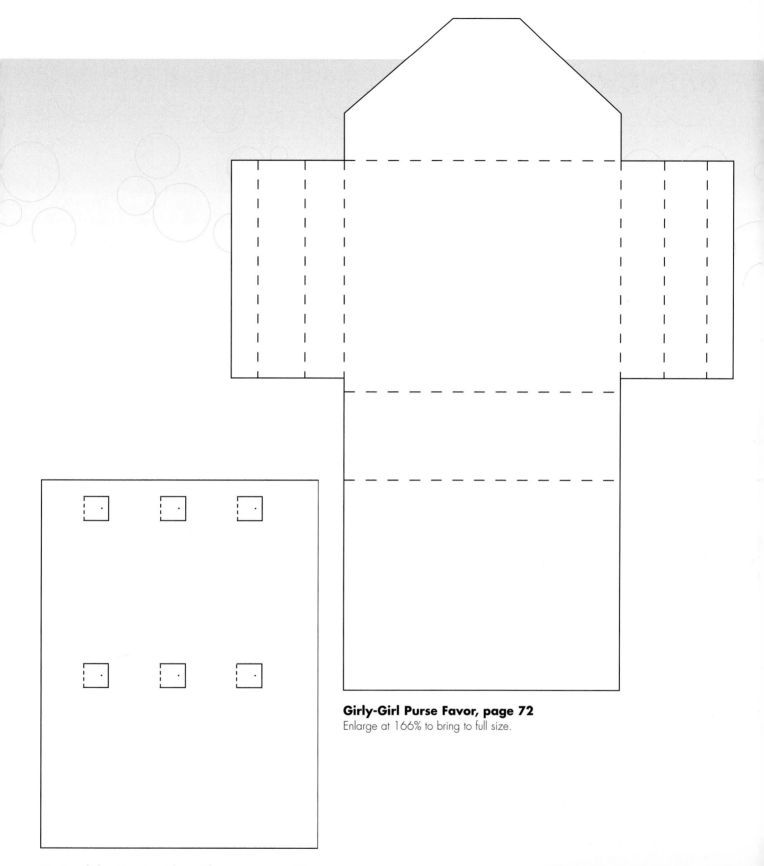

Girly-Girl Purse Favor, page 72
Enlarge at 166% to bring to full size.

Taste of the Tropics Glass Charms, page 36
Enlarge at 143% to bring to full size.

RESOURCES

The products used in this book can be found at your local arts and craft,
scrapbook or rubber stamp store. If you can't find a particular item locally,
contact the manufacturer below for more information.

Papers

Anna Griffin
733 Lambert Dr., Atlanta, GA 30324
888-817-8170
www.annagriffin.com

Autumn Leaves
14140 Ventura Blvd #202, Sherman Oaks, CA 91423
800-588-6707
www.autumnleaves.com
7Gypsies and Rhonna Farrer papers, alphabet rub-ons

Carolee's Creations
3339 N US Highway 91, Hyde Park, UT 84318
435-563-1100
www.caroleescreations.com

Chatterbox
2141 W Beacon Light Rd, Eagle, ID 83616
888-416-6260
www.chatterboxinc.com

Creative Imaginations
17832 Gothard St, Huntington Beach, CA 92647
800-942-6487
www.cigift.com

Deluxe Designs
PO Box 8283, Mesa, AZ 85214
480-497-9005
www.deluxedesigns.com

Doodlebug Designs
2181 W California Ave, Salt Lake City, UT 84104
801-952-0555
www.doodlebug.ws
flower-shaped eyelets

Karen Foster Design
623 N 1250 W, Centerville, UT 84014
801-451-9779
www.karenfosterdesign.com

KI Memories
3720 Arapaho Rd, Addison, TX 75001
972-243-5595
www.kimemories.com

Leisure Arts
5701 Ranch Dr, Little Rock, AR 72223
800-526-5111
www.leisurearts.com

Mara-Mi
1515 Central Ave NE, Minneapolis, MN 55413
800-627-2648
www.mara-mi.com

Masterpiece Studios
2080 Lookout Dr, N Mankato, MN 56003
800-639-7986
www.masterpiecestudios.com

Mustard Moon
918 Schoolhouse Rd, San Jose, CA 95138
408-229-8542
www.mustardmoon.com

Paper Adventures
901 South 5th St, Milwaukee, WI 53204
800-727-0699
www.paperadventures.com

Paper Patch
PO Box 217, West Jordan, UT 84084
801-280-4300
www.paperpatch.com

Rusty Pickle
3945 Wasatch Blvd, Salt Lake City, UT 84124
801-746-1045
www.rustypickle.com

SEI
1717 S 450 W, Logan, UT 84321
435-752-4142
www.shopsei.com

Wordsworth
3725 Cottage Dr, Colorado Springs, CO 80920
719-282-3495
www.wordsworthstamps.com

Embellishments

American Crafts
476 N 1500 W, Orem, UT 84057
801-226-0747
www.americancrafts.com
large monogram stickers

Bisous
89-720 Avonwick Ave, Mississauga, Ontario L5R 4C6, Canada
905-502-7209
www.bisousscrapbooks.com
fashion cutouts

Boxer Scrapbook Productions
22350 SW Grahams Ferry Rd, Tualatin, OR 97062
888-625-6255
www.boxerscrapbooks.com
library pocket and card

EK Success
www.eksuccess.com
Jolee's key charm, silverware

Making Memories
1168 W 500 N, Centerville, UT 84014
801-294-0430
www.makingmemories.com
foam alphabet stamps, pink safety pins, brads

Memory Shoppe, LLC
1509 S Louisville Dr
Columbia, MO 65203
573-289-4922
www.memoryshoppe.com
cocktail stickers

Nunn Design
P.O. Box 906
Port Townsend, WA 98368
360-379-3557

Rubber Stamps

Hero Arts
1343 Powell St, Emeryville, CA 94608
800-822-4376
www.heroarts.com

Hot Potatoes
2805 Columbine Place, Nashville, TN 37204
615-269-8002
www.hotpotatoes.com

Judikins
17803 S Harvard Blvd, Gardena, CA 90248
310-515-1115
www.judikins.com

Rubber Stampede
800-423-4135
www.rubberstampede.com

Tools and Supplies

Bestcontainers.com
Alpine Dynamics
10939 N Alpine Hwy, Ste 510, Highland, UT 84003
www.bestcontainers.com
paint can

Colorbox
Clearsnap, Inc.
PO Box 98, Anacortes, WA 98221
888-448-4862
www.clearsnap.com
chalk ink pads

JudiKins
see contact information under Rubber Stamps
Roxs colored metal flakes, Black Diamond embossing powder, shrink plastic, Diamond Glaze dimensional adhesive

Pacer Technology
9420 Santa Anita Ave, Rancho Cucamonga, CA 91730
800-538-3091
www.pacertech.com
Zap-a-Gap waterproof super glue

Plaid Enterprises
3225 Westech Dr, Norcross, GA 30092
800-842-4197
www.plaidonline.com
Pop-dots dimensional adhesive dots

iNDEX

FIND CREATIVE INSPIRATION AND INSTRUCTION IN OTHER FINE NORTH LIGHT BOOKS!

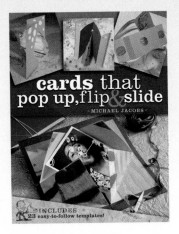

Learn how to craft one-of-a-kind greetings with moving parts such as pop-ups, sliders and flaps. Choose from 22 step-by-step projects that use a variety of papers—from handmade and printed to recycled—to create unique graphic looks. You'll be inspired to jazz up all of your cards with the fun and easy techniques in this book, including using inks, collage and colored pencils in fresh new ways.

ISBN 1-58180-596-9
paperback
96 pages
33109

Whether you're a complete beginner or a seasoned crafter, *Simply Beautiful Greeting Cards* shows you how to create 50 different personalized greeting cards for every occasion. You'll find cards that are great for holidays, birthdays, weddings and "just because." Includes a helpful section on basic tools and materials as well as a treasure trove of papercrafting tips and tricks.

ISBN 1-58180-564-0
paperback
128 pages
33019

MaryJo McGraw brings the hottest scrapbooking techniques to the world of handcrafted cards. She makes it fun and easy for papercrafters and scrapbookers to craft creative, elegant cards using 3-D embellishments. With 26 step-by-step projects and more than 40 variations to choose from, crafters of all skill levels will find inspiration.

ISBN 1-58180-628-0
paperback
128 pages
33201

Designed to inspire friends to gather around the table, break out the projects and create with abandon, *Wild with a Glue Gun* offers a stunning array of craft projects, while showing craft clubs and other small groups how to foster an atmosphere of creative sharing.

ISBN 1-58180-472-5
paperback
144 pages
32740

THESE BOOKS AND OTHER FINE TITLES ARE AVAILABLE FROM YOUR LOCAL ART & CRAFT RETAILER, BOOKSTORE OR ONLINE SUPPLIER.